JUST LIKE US

FOUR SHORT PLAYS FOR LARGE CASTS
BILL TORDOFF

HEINEMANN
SPOTLIGHTS

Heinemann Educational

Heinemann Educational Books Ltd
Halley Court, Jordan Hill, Oxford OX2 8EJ

LONDON   EDINBURGH   MELBOURNE   AUCKLAND
SINGAPORE   KUALA LUMPUR   NEW DELHI
NAIROBI   JOHANNESBURG   IBADAN
KINGSTON   PORTSMOUTH (NH)

ISBN 0 435 23902 3

CAUTION

Typeset by Taurus Graphics
Printed and bound in Great Britain by
Richard Clay Ltd, Bungay, Suffolk

CONTENTS

INTRODUCTION

Like the plays in *Play It For Laughs* and *Laughter Lines*, the four short plays in this collection were all written to give a whole class the fun of putting on a play together. (Alternatively they can be used as the basis of work in Drama, or for reading.) Although some parts are more important than others, all of the characters have individual speeches as well as lines spoken as one of a group. *Just Like Us* is a fairly serious play, but the other three are all comedies.

Apart from *Classjack*, the plays are set in the past. Most of the characters and the plots are, of course, my own invention. I've pointed out the main historical inaccuracies in the forewords to *Just Like Us* and *After 'Astings*. As for *New World*, no-one needs telling that the waves of tourists didn't hit Spain till nearly 500 years after Columbus. However, most of what the sailors tell their girls about their adventures in the West Indies is true, as well as the details of the off-stage procession with Columbus and the King and Queen.

Notes For Novice Directors

Preparation

First write to the publisher for permission to perform the play. Then feel free to change it to suit the size of your cast: you can increase or decrease the number of parts by sharing out the lines differently. You will almost certainly need to re-allocate parts between the sexes, changing names as appropriate. And make sure that you work out moves and groupings before you start rehearsals, even if you have to modify them later.

Acting

In large-cast plays, only a few of the cast will be speaking at any given time. As director, you need to remind them that acting means not just saying lines but remaining in part throughout. (When not speaking, actors will not go far wrong if they look at whoever is speaking, their expressions showing their reactions).

Lines allocated in the script to a group can, of course, be broken up and spoken by different members in performance, and when an individual line is spoken by one of a group, it helps to draw the audience's attention if the actor moves slightly before speaking.

Learning a part

Once the cast know how to say their lines and when to move, they can learn their parts. They need to speak clearly and with feeling, on cue and with the appropriate moves, and they must learn not only their own individual lines but also the lines or choruses spoken by their group.

Later rehearsals

Throughout rehearsals your actors need to speak as loudly as in performance. To ensure this, conduct later rehearsals from the back of the room.

Once scripts are down, rehearsals should begin to approximate to performance. In plays of more than one scene, practise going straight from one to another, striking and setting scenery and props very quickly. If the production is to go smoothly, it is vital that properties (or substitutes) are used in rehearsals: actors need constant practice both to remember lines and to cope with props such as the crown in *After 'Astings*, Dennis's scarf in *Just Like Us*, the different letters in *Classjack* and the food and the signs near the end of *New World*.

Above all, keep reminding yourself that despite the inevitable difficulties and frustrations in rehearsals, it is all worthwhile. There are few feelings more pleasant for both the director and the actors than the elation (and relief!) when the cast take their final curtain call.

B.T.

Just Like Us

CHARACTERS

TEACHER 1★
TEACHER 2★
RADIO VOICE

Vaccies
ALBIE
BERNARD
ERIC
ALAN
BILLY
MICHAEL

ROSIE
GLORIA
MAY
MARY
ALMA
BRENDA

Villagers
DAVID
TOMMY
JOHNNY
JIMMY
BRIAN
HAROLD
DENNIS

BARBARA
LIZZIE
JOAN
JEAN
NANCY
RUTH
MARGARET

TIME: September 1939
SCENE 1: A school in East London
SCENES 2 & 3: A country school

★*Teachers*
As it is hard for children to play the parts of adults while others are playing children, the parts of TEACHER 1 and TEACHER 2 are written so that they can either be acted partly on stage or represented throughout as off-stage voices.

Doubling
Most of the characters are in pairs (MAY and MARY, JOAN and JEAN, etc.) and the size of cast may be reduced by making a pair into one character.

Clothing
Jeans were not worn in England at this time, and boys did not wear long trousers until they were about 13.

Historical Inaccuracies
It is true that 1½ million, mainly children, were evacuated in the three days before Great Britain declared war on Germany in September 1939, but schools did not open for several weeks, and 3 September, when war was declared, was in fact a Sunday.

The Evacuees by B. S. Johnson (Gollancz, 1968) is an anthology of the contributors' experiences of evacuation. For racial prejudice, see the accounts by Gloria Cigman and Ruth Fainlight.

Properties
Gasmask boxes (VACCIES)
Luggage (VACCIES)
Coloured pencil and label (MICHAEL)
Pocket watch (ERIC)
Small model plane (JOHNNY)
Clothes line (NANCY)
Wooden chairs   LIZZIE, BARBARA, GLORIA,
Boxes   ROSIE, JOAN, JEAN
Sweets in a bag (ROSIE)
New scarf (DENNIS)
Bullets, aircraft fragments (CHILDREN)
Pistol (ERIC)

Sound Effects
Warning siren
All-clear siren
Single-engined propeller-driven plane
Steam engine: whistling, starting, moving away

City traffic
Birdsong
Farmyard noises
Bang (plane crash-landing)
Thunder
Pig screaming
Whistle
Handbell
(Most of these are available on tape, or the cast can produce their own and tape them.)

Notes on some Characters
ALBIE, DAVID, TOMMY, NANCY and RUTH are assertive.
ROSIE, GLORIA, LIZZIE and BARBARA are lively and friendly.
BRENDA, ALMA and MARGARET are quiet.
ALAN is quiet and slow-moving.
DENNIS is slow.
MICHAEL is a joker.
JOAN and JEAN are spiteful.
ERIC is a quiet Austrian boy.

German Pronunciation
'Messerschmitt' was almost invariably pronounced by English children as *Meshershmitt*, and is accordingly printed as such. Similarly, 'Nazi' was usually pronounced *Nazzy*, and is so spelled in the text. (Eric knows how to pronounce it. Winston Churchill pronounced it *Narzy*.)

'Junkers' was usually pronounced as written.

Words in 'Die Lorelei'
Weiss: *vice*; Was: *vass*; Soll: *zoll*; Bedeuten: *bedoiten*; Traurig: *trowrik*.

Scene 1

We hear the noise of city traffic, then the voices of children singing. The traffic noise fades as the singing gets louder.

CLASS (*off*): All things bright and beautiful,
                All creatures great and small,
                All things wise and wonderful,
                The Lord God made them all.

The curtain opens. The town class (VACCIES) are standing in rows. On the floor, each has a case or haversack and a cardboard gasmask box on a string. (ERIC'S case is large, with several stick-on labels.) Also on the floor, some have coats with large named luggage-labels fastened to the front, and a few have a cap or beret. The ones without a coat have their label on the string of their gasmask box.

CLASS: The tall trees in the greenwood,
        The meadows where we play,
        The rushes by the water,
        We gather every day.

        All things bright and beautiful,
        All creatures great and small,
        All things wise and wonderful,
        The Lord God made them all.   Amen.

TEACHER 1: That was very nicely sung, children. Mary, call the Jewish children in.

MARY (*by the door*): Miss says you've to come in.

MARY smiles at ROSIE and GLORIA as they enter, followed by ALBIE and ERIC. (Their luggage is already in the room.)

TEACHER 1: Come in quickly, children!

They take their places among the OTHERS, who have begun to chatter.

TEACHER 1: Quiet! Stand still, everybody! Little soldiers! Albie Goldstein, stand still! I want to hear a pin drop! That's better! Now sit quietly. *Quietly*, I said. Up again! Try again! That's better. Today we're going to have another evacuation practice.

CLASS: Aw!

TEACHER 1: Quiet! Have you all got your luggage?

CLASS: Yes, miss!

TEACHER 1: And your gasmasks?

CLASS: Yes, miss!

TEACHER 1: And a large label with your name on?

CLASS: Yes, miss!

TEACHER 1: Good! Michael Morgan, where is your label?

MICHAEL (*pulling a face and holding up a blank label*): Here, miss.

TEACHER 1: Why is there no name on that label? Why do you have to be different from everybody else?

MICHAEL: Miss, 'cause if anybody wants to know my name, I can tell 'em.

TEACHER 1: Stop answering back! Write your name on and tie it on like the others! Now, I'm going to see if the other classes are ready, and I don't want to hear a sound from this room.

MICHAEL *is mimicking her.*

TEACHER 1: Michael Morgan, do you hear?

MICHAEL: Yes, miss.

TEACHER 1: Good. I shan't be long.

The door shuts. MICHAEL *writes on his label with a coloured pencil. The* CLASS *sit quietly, then relax.* SOME *may stand during the following.*

ALBIE: Hey, Bernie, what are meadows supposed to be?

BERNARD: What?

ALBIE: Meadows. In that song you were all singing, it says 'The meadows where we play'.

BERNARD: Must be another word for streets, like where you play football.

MAY: Meadows are like a rec, twerp!

ALAN: A wreck! You mean like an old wrecked car?

GLORIA: No! A recreation ground, with swings and all that.

MARY: I read a story about a girl who gets chased by a bull in a meadow.

BRENDA: Bulls and cows have big horns, don't they?
MAY: I don't think cows chase you.
GLORIA: You get milk from cows.
BERNARD: We don't. We get it from our milkman.

MOST *agree.*

GLORIA: Well, where does he get it from?
BERNARD: Factory.
GLORIA: Stupid! He gets it from cows. They have it in their bags.

SOME: *giggle.*

MICHAEL: Three bags of milk, please!

Laughter

ROSIE: Another thing. In that song, why do you all sing about
   Russians? 'Cause my grandad comes from Russia.
ALL: Russians?
MAY: What are you talking about?
ROSIE (*singing*): 'The Russians by the water
                    We gather every day.'

Laughter.

MAY: It's not 'Russians': it's 'rushes', you twerp!
ROSIE: Well, what are rushes?

   ALL: *look blank and shrug.*

ROSIE: You don't know, do you?
MICHAEL: Never mind about rushes, why are we waiting
   around?
ALL: Yeah!
GLORIA: What time is it, Eric?
ERIC: (*taking out a fob-watch*): Ten hours. Ten o'clock.
BILLY: Cor! That's a posh watch!
ERIC: My father gave it to me when I was sick.
ROSIE: Well, I'm sick of all these evacuation practices. It's all right
   for you, Alma, you missed the others, didn't you?
ALMA: Yes, but I know I shall cry.

ROSIE: Cry? What for?

ALMA: 'Cause I'm scared of having a needle stuck in me. I cried last time.

ALL: (*jeering*): Aw!

BRENDA: We're not going to be vaccinated, Alma: we're going to be *evacuated*.

ALMA: What?

ALL: Evacuated!

ALMA: Well, what do they do to you?

ALL *groan*

BRENDA: They don't do anything to you! We all walk down to the station.

ALBIE: And then we all walk back. We practised three times last week, didn't we?

ALL: Yeah!

ALMA: Why?

BILLY: 'Cos when the war starts, the Germans'll drop bombs on London, so we all have to get away on a train.

ALAN: Oh, smashing! I've never been on a train! You been on a train, Eric?

ALL *look at* ERIC, *who nods*.

ALAN: How far did you go? A long way?

ERIC *nods again*.

ALBIE: Leave him alone.

BRENDA: My dad says we'll be going today because the war'll start tomorrow. That's why we all have to have our cases packed.

ALMA: Where do we all go to on this train?

ALL *look round at each other and shrug*.

MARY: We go where we shan't get bombed and gassed. Then we come home again.

BILLY: We go to the country.

BRENDA: Which country?

BILLY: Where it's meadows and that.

ALMA: There might be cows. I'd rather go to the seaside. We went to Southend once.

GLORIA: My father says we'll go to Scotland.

MICHAEL: Och aye, the noo!

Laughter

ALAN: Perhaps we'll go to Australia, where Eric comes from.

MICHAEL: Yeah! Then we can throw boomerangs at kangaroos!

Laughter.

MAY: He's not from Australia, you twerp! He's from Austria. Aren't you, Eric? See!

ALMA: What's he want to come here for?

MAY: 'Cos the Nazzies are in Austria.

ALMA: What are Nazzies?

MAY: It's another word for Germans, like Jerries.

ALMA: Did you come with your mum?

ERIC *nods.*

ALMA: And your dad?

ERIC *shakes his head.*

ALBIE: The Nazzies took his father away and put him in prison.

ALMA: Why? Is he a burglar?

ERIC: No, he is a doctor. They came to our house in the night with guns and took him away because he is Jewish.

MARY: They must be stupid! You might as well put people in jail because they're English.

BERNARD: Or Irish.

ALAN: Where we go on this train, they might put us in prison just for being English.

Laughter.

ALBIE: You twerp! They'll be English as well, won't they? Just like us.

ALAN: I don't know.

ERIC: Will there also be Jewish people where we go on the train, like in London?

MARY: I suppose so.

ERIC: In Austria and in Poland, some people hate the Jews.

MARY: Don't worry, Eric: they'll be just like us.

BERNARD (*grinning*): They might hate Albie Goldstein 'cos he's a big-head.

ALBIE: Better than being stupid!

ALBIE *and* BERNARD *wrestle while the* OTHERS *cheer or complain.*

BRENDA: Teacher! Teacher!

ALL *sit quietly.*

TEACHER 1: I hope I didn't hear any chattering from this room, did I?

ALL: No, miss!

TEACHER 1: Good. Now, we're off to the station again.

ALL: Aw, no!

TEACHER 1: Quiet! Michael Morgan, have you written your name on your label?

MICHAEL (*singsong*): Yes, miss!

BERNARD (*raising a hand*): Miss, Michael Morgan has written 'Mickey Mouse' on his label.

Laughter.

TEACHER 1: Quiet! Quiet! Michael Morgan, you are a silly show-off! Now, while I call the register, I want you to put on your coats. *When* I say the word! Make sure your labels are firmly tied on, pick up your gasmask and luggage and line up, boys first, in alphabetical order. You know what that means?

ALL: Yes, miss!

TEACHER 1: Right. Get ready. *Quietly.*

As the TEACHER *reads the register,* ALL *do as she says, each answering to his/her name.*

TEACHER 1: Alan Brown, Eric Fischer, Albie Goldstein, Michael

Morgan, Bernard O'Donnell, Billy Watson, Gloria Cohen,
Brenda Fogarty, Rosie Greenberg, Mary McAskie, May
Morton, Alma Thorpe.

ROSIE: Miss, are we really going on a train this time?
TEACHER 1: Perhaps. You'll see.

A warning siren starts up. ALL *start talking.*

TEACHER 1: Quiet! That is just a practice siren. Now stand
quietly until I come and lead you to the station.

ALL *stand motionless. The lights might dim slightly here.*

RADIO VOICE: Here is the morning news. German forces are
reported to be thrusting deeper into Poland, in spite of
determined Polish resistance. Strong armoured columns . . . .

The VOICE *and the siren fade into the background as* MICHAEL
speaks.

MICHAEL: Hey! What are the Poles doing in Russia?
BERNARD: I don't know, what are the Poles doing in Russia?
MICHAEL: Holding the telegraph wires up. Get it? Poles!

ALL *groan.*

TEACHER 1: Michael Morgan! I'm not going to tell you again!

The siren becomes audible again.

RADIO VOICE: The Prime Minister announced in the House of
Commons yesterday that unless we receive a reply today from
the German government to the British and French demands to
cease hostilities against Poland, then we shall be at war with
Germany!

The siren runs down.

TEACHER 1: That was just a practice alarm, children. What was
it?
ALL: Just a practice, miss.
TEACHER 1: Good. Are we all ready?
ALL: Yes, miss.

TEACHER 1: Good. Heads up! Little soldiers! Quick march! Left, right! Left, right! Off we march to the station! Left, right! Left, right!

    ALL *march round the stage, singing*:

ALL: Whistle while you work!
    Hitler is a twerp!
    He's half barmy,
    So's his army,
    Whistle while you work!

    ALL *march off, humming or whistling the tune, while we hear an engine whistle and the sound of a steam-train slowly starting and chuffing away, giving a final whistle as it fades.*

Scene 2

Birdsong and farmyard noises. A handbell rings and we hear a burst of children's voices. There is a noise like an approaching plane, then JOHNNY *enters holding up a small metal fighter-plane and making the plane noise. Enter* DAVID *and* TOMMY.

DAVID (*grabbing the plane*): You lucky devil! Where d'you get this?
TOMMY: That's a Hawker Hurricane, innit?
JOHNNY: Give us it, David Clancey! It's a Spitfire.
DAVID: I didn't know planes could spit.

    He spits on the plane.

JOHNNY: Give up!
DAVID: You pinched it, kid, didn't you?

    He 'flies' the plane.

JOHNNY: I didn't! My mum bought it me. She went to Oxton on the Tuesday bus.
DAVID: Here!

    He throws the plane back. JOHNNY *wipes it.*

TOMMY: I never been to Oxton. I bet it's stupid.

Enter DENNIS. *He is shabby and wears an old scarf.*

DAVID: Yeah, like Dennis.

DENNIS: I ain't stupid.

TOMMY: What are we going to play at?

DAVID: English and Germans. Dennis can be a German 'cos he
stinks.

DENNIS (*sniffing himself*): Been mucking the pigs out, haven't I?

TOMMY: You always stink. Don't come no nearer.

JOHNNY: 'Cos we haven't got our gasmasks.

DENNIS: Girls are coming.

Enter the VILLAGE GIRLS. NANCY *has a length of
clothesline.*

NANCY: Move, you boys!

TOMMY: Why should we?

RUTH: 'Cos we want to skip, that's why.

GIRLS: Yeah!

DAVID: We was here first, and we want to play English and
Jerries.

NANCY: You can play that anywhere. (*Pointing*) There's the
meadow! There's the woods! Move, Dennis!

The GIRLS *bustle into the centre of the stage and the* BOYS
reluctantly drift to one side. NANCY *and* RUTH *turn the rope and
the* GIRLS *skip through, chanting*:

GIRLS: Charlie Chaplin went to France
      To teach little French girls how to dance.
      First they did the wibble-wobbles,
      Then they did the kicks,
      Then they did the can–can,
      Then they did the splits.

DAVID (*looking off-stage*): Here come the Jerries, men! Get down
and let 'em have it!

HAROLD, JIMMY *and* BRIAN *sneak on and start 'machine-
gunning' the* OTHERS, *who fire back. There is pandemonium as the*
GIRLS *all chant and the* BOYS *all 'fire'.* DAVID *finally goes up to*

the 'JERRIES', *including* DENNIS, *and 'shoots' them, saying
'You're dead'. They lie down. He pretends to take a gun from each. The*
GIRLS *start to skip with their backs to the audience and their voices
grow quieter.*

DAVID: We've won! The English are best!

DENNIS (*jumping up and 'shooting' him*): Bang! You're dead!

DAVID: Lie down, stupid: you haven't got no gun.

DENNIS (*lying down*): Aw.

DAVID: You're all dead till you've counted 100.

One after another the BOYS *count the last few numbers up to* 100
and stand. DENNIS *chants gibberish then shouts 'A hundred!' and
stands.*

TOMMY: Let's start again.

BRIAN: No, it's boring, always playing English and Jerries.

BOYS: Yeah.

JIMMY: The war's started. It was on the wireless.

DENNIS: My uncle says when they come here they'll shoot us,
them Germs.

BOYS: Germans.

DENNIS: Same difference.

HAROLD: Germans won't come here.

JIMMY: My dad says vaccies is coming.

BRIAN: What's vaccies?

JIMMY: Dunno.

HAROLD: Evacuees.

JIMMY: Well, whatever they are, my dad says they'll take over if
we don't stop 'em.

DAVID: Vaccies must be like Jerries, then. We'll have to fight 'em.

BOYS: Let's play English and vaccies, then. Who wants to be a
vaccy?

Silence.

BRIAN: Girls could be vaccies.

BOYS: Yeah!

DAVID (*shouting and shooting*): Get the vaccies!

BOYS: Get the vaccies!

The BOYS *advance chanting on the* GIRLS, *who stop skipping
and stare.*

LIZZIE: What's wrong with you?

BRIAN: We're English fighting vaccies.

BARBARA: You're all stupid.

GIRLS: Yeah!

BRIAN: What are we stupid for?

BARBARA: Vaccies *are* English, 'cos they live in England.

JIMMY: No, they don't. They live in London.

MARGARET: Well, London's England, isn't it?

TOMMY: It isn't.

MARGARET: It is.

TOMMY: 'Tisn't.

ALL *take sides in a crescendo of "'Tis' and "'Tisn't' until a whistle
blows.*

TEACHER 2 (*off*): What is all this silly noise about? Just play
quietly till the end of playtime. I'm watching you, David
Clancey.

DAVID: Yes, miss.

JEAN: Our mam says vaccies have never seen no cows.

RUTH: Are they all blind, then?

MARGARET: 'Course they're not!

RUTH: Well, why haven't they seen no cows, then?

MARGARET: 'Cos they haven't no fields, have they? It's all
houses in London and them places. My aunty went.

DENNIS: Well, if these vaccies have got houses in London, what
do they want to come here for?

Silence. Shrugs.

HAROLD: My dad says they eat something called bubble-and-
squeak.

JOHNNY: Bubble and squeak! Sounds like pig-swill!

Laughter.

JOAN: Our mam says they live like pigs. She says this vaccy went
to live in this house where they had a carpet on the floor. And

you know what this vaccy did? He wet it!

TOMMY: Here, I bet their houses don't half smell!

NANCY: I bet Dennis is a vaccy, 'cos he smells.

Laughter.

DAVID: Come on, let's play English and vaccies!

LIZZIE: How do you play it?

DAVID: Shooting!

GIRLS: Oh, no!

BOYS: Yes!

GIRLS: No!

TOMMY: Well, how else can we play it?

Silence.

JOAN: I know! Like Blindman's Buff. We get in a ring, and one's blindfolded, and somebody says 'Vaccy, vaccy!' and if the one what's on can touch 'em, then they're the vaccy.

ALL: Yeah!

NANCY: Who's first vaccy?

ALL: Dennis!

TOMMY *and* BRIAN *grab him and blindfold him with his scarf while he says 'Get off!'*

JOAN: Make a ring!

ALL *make a ring, open on the downstage side.*

JOAN (*to* DENNIS): If you touch anybody, you say this: (*She whispers to him*) Right!

JOAN *spins* DENNIS.

JEAN: Vaccy, vaccy!

DENNIS *moves towards her, but she creeps behind him and pushes him, shouting 'Vaccy!'. HAROLD repeats this, then more than one calls out, so that DENNIS blunders round as they call and push. Enter the VACCIES, still carrying luggage and wearing their labels. They stay in one corner in a tight bunch, watching. As the VILLAGERS see them, they gradually stop, whispering 'Vaccies!' At last ALL are silent and still, except* DENNIS, *who gropes around until he touches* ALBIE, *shouts 'Smelly vaccy!' and removes his blindfold. Then he says 'Oo!' in surprise and looks round.* ALL *are staring at him. He reads* ALBIE'S *label aloud: 'Albie', then gives him the scarf and says 'You're on'.*

BARBARA: Are you playing?

    ALBIE *looks round, shrugs, and nods.*

BARBARA: Stand in the middle, then.

    ALBIE *puts down his luggage and stands in the middle.*

JEAN (*stepping forward*): You have to touch the one who calls out, then you say 'Smelly vaccy'.
ALBIE: Say what?
VILLAGERS: Smelly vaccy!
JEAN: You know what that means?

    ALBIE *shakes his head and* SOME VILLAGERS *laugh.*

JEAN: You'll soon find out!

    She blindfolds him and spins him.

ALBIE (*to himself*): Smellyvaccy, smellyvaccy.

    DAVID *holds up his arms for silence, then tiptoes behind* ALBIE. *He taps him on the shoulder, says 'Vaccy!' and leaps back. The* VILLAGERS *laugh. Again* DAVID *taps him and jumps back, and the* VILLAGERS *laugh louder. The third time,* ALBIE *is ready. As* DAVID *taps him, he grabs his wrist with both hands and pulls him forward over his head.* ALL *exclaim as* DAVID *yells, falls, and lies winded.* SOME *laugh or applaud.* ALBIE *takes off the scarf, holds it out, smiling, to* DAVID *as he rises and says 'Smellyvaccy'.* DAVID *scowls and snatches it. A handbell rings.*

MARGARET: End of playtime. (*Pointing*) Go in that door.

    The VACCIES *look where she is pointing, pick up their things and go out.* ERIC *and* ALBIE *are the last off.*

DAVID: I'll get one of you stinking vaccies, just you wait!

ERIC *and* ALBIE *turn and stare, then go out. A whistle sounds and the* VILLAGERS *stand in two lines,* GIRLS *and* BOYS. *Another whistle; they march out,* GIRLS *first.*

Scene 3

Enter LIZZIE, BARBARA, GLORIA, ROSIE, JOAN *and* JEAN *carrying wooden chairs and boxes.*

TEACHER 2 (*off*): Leave them there! That's right! We'll move them back after playtime, when we've finished cleaning the store-room.

ROSIE: Want a sweet?

LIZZIE (*after a slight hesitation*): Thanks. What do they call you?

ROSIE: Rosie. Gloria's my friend, aren't you, Gloria?

LIZZIE: I'm Lizzie. This is Barbara. That's Joan and Jean.

GLORIA: Are you two sisters?

JOAN *and* JEAN *nod, blank-faced.*

GLORIA: I thought you were.

ROSIE: Have a sweet.

BARBARA *takes one and says 'Thank you'.* JOAN *and* JEAN *shake their heads.*

ROSIE: Go on!

They each take one, still silent and staring.

LIZZIE: You like it down here?

GLORIA: It's all right. I miss my mum and dad, though.

LIZZIE: Do you, Rosie?

ROSIE: Yes. I wish I could go home. Some people are nice, but I hate some of those boys. They were calling us names last night.

BARBARA: That's David Clancey and his gang. They shout at us as well. They're just stupid.

LIZZIE: You should hear David Clancey's dad when he gets drunk. Last Saturday he was shouting and cursing in the street and hitting David and his brother.

GLORIA: And it's usually so quiet round here, isn't it?

Suddenly there is a shrill, prolonged screaming. GLORIA *grabs* ROSIE *while the* OTHERS *laugh.*

GLORIA: ⎫
          ⎬ What is it?
ROSIE: ⎭

JOAN: That's Johnny Larcomb's dad, isn't it?

ROSIE: It doesn't sound like a man. Is he hurt?

JEAN: It's a pig. He's killing it, isn't he?

ROSIE: Why? What's it done?

   The VILLAGE GIRLS *laugh.*

BARBARA: It's just got fat enough to eat. He's the butcher. You like pork?

   ROSIE *shakes her head.*

GLORIA: She's a Jew.

JOAN: Ooh, that's an awful thing to say when she's your friend! She doesn't cheat people, do you, Rosie?

GLORIA: No, I just mean she's Jewish. So am I. And Albie. Eric Fischer is as well.

JEAN: Are you *Jews*?

   ROSIE *and* GLORIA *nod.* JOAN *and* JEAN *look at each other and edge away.*

BARBARA: You can't be, 'cos you talk English.

ROSIE: Yes, but . . . . Aren't there any Jewish people in this village?

   The VILLAGE GIRLS *shake their heads.*

ROSIE: Well, do you go to church?

BARBARA: Sometimes. We all go from school on Ascension Day.

ROSIE: We don't go to church: we go to a synagogue.

   JEAN *and* JOAN *stare at each other.* JOAN *whispers to* JEAN.

ROSIE: We can't go into a church, and we're not supposed to sing hymns or join in prayers at school.

GLORIA: Or eat pork.

ROSIE: Or eat pork. When the others say prayers or learn about Jesus and that, we just wait in another room, unless our Rabbi comes.

JOAN: What's one of them?

ROSIE: A sort of Jewish vicar.

LIZZIE: Well, there isn't another room here, except that store-room. Where will you go when it's snowing?

ROSIE *and* GLORIA *shrug.*

BARBARA: You can't sit outside in the toilets: you'll freeze. You ought to stay inside with the rest of us.

GLORIA: We shouldn't do that. Besides, we wouldn't know what to say.

LIZZIE: You just sing from the hymnbook with us. Oh, and say the Lord's Prayer.

GLORIA: We don't know that.

JOAN *and* JEAN *suddenly whisper to each other, glare at the* OTHERS *and march out.*

GLORIA: What's wrong with them?

BARBARA: Take no notice of 'em. They're always sulking about something.

MARY *and* MAY *run in moaning.*

ROSIE: What's the matter?

MARY: It's raining.

MAY: Cats and dogs.

The OTHERS *hurry in, shaking the rain off and chattering. The* VILLAGERS *and* VACCIES *tend to stay apart, but there is some intermingling.*

LIZZIE: Shhh! She'll send us out in the rain!

ALMA: It's getting dark: I hope it doesn't thunder. I hate storms.

Thunder rumbles and ALMA *moans.*

DENNIS: You hold your hush. You sound like a ghost.

HAROLD: How do you know what a ghost sounds like?

DENNIS: 'Cos I do, see?

MAY: I don't believe in ghosts.

ROSIE: I don't either.

NANCY: We do, don't we?

VILLAGERS: Yeah.

JOAN: I seen one in the graveyard. We both did. Didn't we, Jean?

MAY: What was it like?

JOAN:⎫
JEAN:⎬ Shan't tell you.

BERNARD: Ghosts are stupid.

TOMMY: Like vaccies.

BRENDA: We're not stupid. Anyway, there's no ghosts in London, not where we live.

TOMMY: Maybe not, but don't none of you vaccies go in our churchyard at night, when there's a sickle moon over them old gravestones, 'cos you might meet a ghost, see?

JOAN: Some of 'em can't go in that churchyard day or night. Or in the church.

BRIAN: 'Course they can. Anybody can go in.

JEAN: Some of 'em can't.

BRIAN: Why not, then?

JEAN: 'Cos they're Jews, that's why.

BRIAN: What do you mean, Jews?

JEAN: They're dirty Jews, and they don't have no church of Jesus: they have a Sinner-God!

DENNIS: A Sinner-God!

GLORIA: It's not 'Sinner-God': it's 'Synagogue'.

HAROLD: Who are you talking about?

JOAN (*pointing*): Her and her. And him. And him. They're all dirty Jews.

ALBIE: We're not dirty. We're cleaner than you and your Jean, at any rate.

Laughter.

JEAN: You shut up! They're not Christians!

JOAN: They don't say their prayers to Jesus Christ in church!

JOHNNY: Well, your dad don't go to church. Nor his (*pointing*), nor hers. What's it matter? Let's stop arguing and play at something. Armies.

GIRLS: Aw, no!

DENNIS (*loud*): My uncle says German army is coming.

JIMMY: Yes. My dad has to paint out the sign over our shop 'cos it has the name of our village on, then the Jerries won't know where they are when they come.

BILLY: They done the same at the station.

ALAN: P'raps when they come they'll think they're in Germany.

HAROLD: No, they'll know they're not, 'cos we don't talk German.

JOHNNY: I bet we could talk some German. We could say 'Ja, ja'.

ALAN: What's 'Ja, ja'?

JOHNNY: It means 'Yes'. They don't say 'Yes', they all say 'Ja, ja'.

ALL (*nodding to each other*): Ja, ja! Ja, ja!

BARBARA: They say 'Nein' as well.

RUTH: So do we: Seven, eight, nine.

BARBARA: Yes, but in German, 'Nein' means 'No'. Doesn't it, Eric?

JOAN: That's stupid.

JOHNNY: Well, I bet they are stupid. We could fool 'em easy. We could all say 'Ja, ja' and 'Nein, nein'.

ALL: Ja, ja! Nein, nein!

MICHAEL: Ten, ten!

Laughter

MARGARET: My dad has a Jerry belt from the Great War, and it says 'Gott mit uns'.

ALL: Gott mit uns. Ja, ja. Nein, nein.

ALBIE: Heinkel!

ALL: Heinkel!

BILLY: Junkers!

ALL: Junkers!

BERNARD: Meshershmitt!

ALL: Meshershmitt!

JOHNNY: Hey, that's smashing! If they come here they'll think we're Germans. Say it again. Ja, ja.

BARBARA: Nein, nein.

MARGARET: Gott mit uns!

ALBIE: Heinkel!

BILLY: Junkers!

BERNARD: Meshershmitt!

ALL: Ja, ja. Nein, nein. Gott mit uns! Heinkel, Junkers,
Meshershmitt!

> *As he says 'Meshershmitt' BERNARD raises his hand in a Nazi salute.*

DAVID: That's what they do! That's it! They do this! (*Saluting*)

ALL: Yeah!

MICHAEL: And they all walk like this!

> *MICHAEL goose-steps, saluting. ALL laugh. He puts two fingers to his upper lip to make a Hitler moustache.*

MICHAEL: Ja, ja! Nein, nein! Gott mit uns! Heinkel, Junkers,
Meshershmitt! Heil, Hitler!

BERNARD (*mock-German, to* DENNIS): Why do you not say
'Heil, Hitler' like the other peoples?

DENNIS: 'Cos I can't talk like them Germs.

ALL: Germans.

DENNIS: Them Germans.

JOAN (*pointing at* ERIC): He wasn't saying it either.

MARY: Oh, leave him alone!

DAVID: Say 'Heil, Hitler', kid.

> ERIC *shakes his head.*

JEAN: He's a Nazzy.

> *Shouts of 'Nazzy!'*

MARY: He's not a Nazzy, are you Eric?

> ERIC *shakes his head.*

JEAN: He must be dumb.

DAVID: Are you dumb, kid? Say some German or I'll bash you.

MARY: Leave him! He doesn't talk much.

ERIC *whispers to* ALBIE.

DAVID: What's he whispering?
ALBIE: He says he'll sing some German for you.

ERIC *whispers again.*

ALBIE: He says it's a song called Lorelei.
JEAN: Is it about Laurel and Hardy?

Laughter.

MAY: Listen to him! Tell 'em, Eric.
ERIC: 'Die Lorelei' is a song about a maiden. She sits on a rock by the river and combs her golden hair.

TOMMY *blows a raspberry.* SOME *laugh.*

GLORIA: Let him sing. Go on, Eric.

ERIC *waits till all are quiet, then sings:*
(*Pronunciation on page 9*)

ERIC: Ich weiss nicht, was soll es bedeuten
Dass ich so traurig bin . . . .

ERIC *stops as* DENNIS *starts to imitate him, 'singing' gibberish.* SOME *laugh.*

ALMA: Let him sing! It's nice.
TOMMY: It's rubbish.
MAY: It isn't then: it's proper German. Sing it again, Eric.

ERIC *shakes his head, close to tears.*

MAY: What did it mean, what you sang?
ERIC: My song says, 'I do not know what it means, that I am so sad'.

ERIC *covers his face. Silence.*

DAVID: We don't want to listen to stupid foreign songs. We've got to be ready to fight the Nazzies when they come. Singing won't help.
TOMMY: We ought to drill, like soldiers.

DAVID: Right! Everybody get in lines, then!

ALL *line up in rows at one side of the stage, facing the audience.*

DAVID: Attention!

ALL *stand to attention.*

DAVID (*pointing at* ERIC): You! Get out! Move over there!
ALBIE: Why should he? What's he done wrong?
DAVID: We don't have no foreigners in the English army. They might be spies.

ERIC *shrugs and crosses the room.*

ALBIE: He's not a foreigner now.
TOMMY: Call him 'sir'.
ALBIE (*rolling his eyes*): He's not a foreigner, *sir*. Not now. You come back, Eric.
DAVID: You stay over there!
BERNARD: Aw, let him play!
DAVID: I'm the boss, and I say he's not English, so he can't be in my army. He's an outsider.
ALBIE: Well, if Eric's an outsider, so am I.

ALBIE *crosses to* ERIC.

JOAN: We ought to kick all them Jews out.

Some VILLAGERS *mutter approval, staring at* ROSIE *and* GLORIA *who look at each other, then cross the room.*

MICHAEL: That's senseless: they're just like us.
DAVID: No! They are different!
MICHAEL: 'Course they're different! I'm different, you're different, everybody's different! (*Pointing*) She's tall, he's small, she's thin, he's fat.
ALAN: I'm not! I'm just well-built.
MICHAEL: All right, you're well-built. (*Pointing again*) He's got black hair, she's got fair. Blue eyes, brown eyes, boys, girls. We're all alike 'cos we're all different!
DAVID: I don't care! I don't like outsiders. I don't like you.

MICHAEL: I don't like you either, but we can still play together, all of us.

DAVID: It's not natural for different kinds to mix.

MICHAEL (*looking out of the window*): What's wrong with all them cows in that field?

DAVID: Nothing's wrong: they're just eating grass.

MICHAEL: That's right. What kind are they? Are they all the same?

The VILLAGERS *laugh.*

DAVID: 'Course they're not the same! Black and white are Friesians, white and red are Shorthorns. Brown are Jerseys, aren't they?

LIZZIE: And what do you call those with black and white sort of smudged?

DAVID: We call them blue.

LIZZIE: So that field is full of cows . . . .

DAVID: Heifers.

LIZZIE: Sorry, heifers: young ones. All mixed up: red, white and blue, black and brown. All just eating grass. I don't notice 'em ganging up on each other 'cos they're different colours, do you?

DAVID: You think you're clever, you! But I don't care what nobody says.

LIZZIE: Are you going to let them come back and play with us?

DAVID: No, I'm not.

LIZZIE: Right. Count me out.

LIZZIE *crosses the room.*

DAVID: Any more traitors before we start drilling?

MICHAEL: Me.

MICHAEL *crosses the room.*

DAVID: Right! Get in rows!

They line up, with TOMMY *helping to align them.*

DAVID: Attention! Stand at ease! Like this. Again! Attention! Stand at ease! Attention! That's good, my army. (*To* TOMMY) What's next?

TOMMY: Saluting, sir.

DAVID: All salute me! Attention! Stand at ease! Attention! Salute! Attention! Rifle drill now.

TOMMY: Chief! Sir! We haven't got no rifles yet.

DAVID: Oh, well, we'll do marching on the spot.

SOME *groan*.

TOMMY: Shut up! All do what the officer says.

BRIAN *starts to cross*.

TOMMY: Where are you going?

BRIAN: It's boring.

SOME *agree*.

DAVID: Come here, kid. Now! You want bashing, kid?

BRIAN: No.

DAVID: Well, get in line. Anybody else drops out gets bashed. What's next?

DENNIS (*raising a hand*): Can we all shout like them Nazzies? It's good fun.

ARMY: Yeah!

DAVID: Right. What are we going to shout?

DENNIS: 'England is bestest'.

TOMMY: Best.

DENNIS: Yeah. 'England is best'.

DAVID: }
TOMMY: } (*chanting*): England is best!

ARMY: Yes!

MARY (*raising a hand*): Do I have to shout it, 'cos my dad comes from Scotland?

DAVID: Er, is Scotland in England, sergeant-major, or is she a traitor?

TOMMY: Er, Scotland is in England, sir.

Some OUTSIDERS *laugh*.

DAVID: Shut up, you outsiders!

ERIC *is still smiling*. DAVID *crosses to him in a rage*.

DAVID: What's funny, traitor?

ERIC: Nothing.

DAVID (*shouting*): What are you laughing at?

ERIC: You say your army is only for the English, but you do not know where England is.

> SOME *laugh*.

DAVID: Stop laughing at me! Nobody laughs at me! If I say Scotland is in England, well it is!

> *He punches* ERIC, *who yells and doubles up, then straightens, takes out his watch and starts crying.*

ALBIE: You've broken his dad's watch.

GIRLS: Aw!

DAVID: And it's not the only thing I'll break if you don't all shut up!

> DAVID *crosses back in silence.*

TOMMY: Right. Marching on the spot. Left, right. Left, right. Left, right. Halt, one, two! Chanting now: 'England is best'.

DAVID: No: just 'England best'.

TOMMY: Right, sir. All marching and chanting! Left, right. Left, right. England best! England best!

> *The* ARMY *march on the spot, chanting, with* DAVID *facing them. Then he turns to face the audience and starts to shout louder and faster than the* OTHERS, *who look at him in a worried way and gradually fall still and silent. They edge away from him and the* OUTSIDERS *join them.* DAVID *begins to punch the air as he chants, then he puts his hands to his head, sways and moans.* ERIC *and* TOMMY *push a chair behind him. He sits, still moaning.* SOME *start to mutter, but* ERIC *raises a hand to quieten them.*

TOMMY: You're all right now, Dave.

> ERIC *strokes* DAVID'S *forehead from behind.*

TOMMY: Your dad been hitting you again, has he, Dave?

DAVID (*nodding*): Batted me on the head. Give me a right headache, he did.

DAVID *puts up a hand and touches* ERIC's, *then looks up to see whose it is. Suddenly the warning siren sounds.* DAVID *stands and* ALL *look and listen. Then* ALAN *sees something high above the audience. He says 'Look!' and points.* ALL *stare. The siren runs down and a single-engined plane can be heard.*

BERNARD: Spitfire!
TOMMY: Hawker Hurricane!
BILLY: It's a Meshershmitt! It's got Nazzy crosses!
ALL: Nazzies!
BRIAN: Look, it's smoking!
JIMMY: It's coming down!

The noise of the plane gets louder. ALL *watch it.*

JOHNNY: He's going to crash-land!
ALL: Yeah!

The noise is very loud. DENNIS *rushes out.* ALL *duck and turn,* SOME *screaming, as it passes overhead. There is a bang.* ALBIE *shouts 'Come on!' and* ALL *run out,* ALAN *last. Outside we hear a cheer which fades. Silence, then a whistle and a handbell.*

TEACHER 2 (*off*): Back to school! All of you! David Clancey! Albie Goldstein! Get away from that aeroplane! Leave it! The policeman's coming!
ALAN (*plodding in*): I never got there, did I?

We hear the CHILDREN *talking excitedly, then they straggle in.*

GLORIA: What have you got?
JOAN (*showing them*): Two bits off the back.
GLORIA: I've got some bullets: look!
ROSIE: So have I.
JOAN: Swap you a bit off the back for a bullet.
GLORIA: All right.
JEAN: Swap you this for six bullets.
GLORIA: Four.
JEAN: Six.
ROSIE: I'll give you five.
JEAN: All right.

ALL *are showing souvenirs and swapping. Enter* DAVID *and* ALBIE.

ALBIE: I swiped the pilot's watch: look!
DAVID: I got his wallet.
ALBIE: Swap!
DAVID (*after hesitating*): All right.
BILLY: Who got his scarf?
BERNARD: He has it!

He points to DENNIS, *who enters wearing a new scarf and grinning.*

JOHNNY: Swap you six bullets for the scarf? Ten?
DENNIS: Bullets don't keep your neck warm.
ALAN: Why did he give you his scarf? Did you ask him?

Laughter.

NANCY: He wasn't moving, was he?
BRENDA: I didn't go near him.

SOME agree.

RUTH: I reckon he knocked his head when he crashed.
JOHNNY: He was starting to move when Miss called out.
DENNIS: He got out after most of you came back here.
DAVID: Liar! Where is he, then?
DENNIS: Eric took his gun and said some foreign words and he put his hands up till the copper came.
DAVID: Liar! He hasn't the guts to take a gun and do that!
ERIC (*in the doorway*): No?

ALL stare as ERIC *crosses to* DAVID, *produces a pistol and offers it to him.*

ERIC: You like guns? Take this! Here!

DAVID *shakes his head.*

ERIC: Take it!
TEACHER 2 (*off*): Eric Fischer! Is that a gun in your hand?
ERIC: Yes, miss.

TEACHER 2 (*off*): You silly little boy! Bring it here this minute!

Exit ERIC. DAVID *replaces the chair.* ERIC *returns.*

DAVID: Did she pinch your gun?

ERIC *nods.*

DAVID: And I broke your watch. (*Holding out the pilot's watch*) Here: it's the pilot's. I only break things.
ERIC (*taking it after a slight hesitation*): Thank you.

DENNIS *starts to clap and the* OTHERS *join in.*

ERIC: Thank you very much.

ERIC *puts on the watch.*

MARGARET: Eric, would you like to finish your song?

The BOYS *groan.*

ERIC: No. That is a sad song. We should sing happy songs, is that right?
ALL: That's right!

The all-clear siren sounds.

ERIC: That is the all-clear: the Nazis have gone. But they will come back, and we must all stand together. So, put your hands on the shoulders of your comrades.

ALL *stand with hands on each other's shoulders.*

ERIC: Good! Now we shall all sing 'Ten Green Flasks'.
ALL: What?
ALAN (*grinning*): You mean 'Ten Green Bottles'.
ERIC (*grinning*): I mean 'Ten Green Bottles'. *He sings*:
ERIC: Ten Nazi pilots flying all around.
ALL (*swaying*): Ten Nazi pilots flying all around.
ERIC But if one Nazi pilot should crash into the ground,
ALL: There'd be nine Nazi pilots flying all around.

The siren runs down.

ERIC: Nine Nazi pilots flying all around.
ALL: Nine Nazi pilots flying all around.
ERIC But if one Nazi pilot should crash into the ground,
ALL: There'd be eight Nazi pilots flying all around.

As they begin the third verse the curtain closes. When it opens again,
ALL *sing the last verse*:

ALL: One Nazi pilot flying all around,
    One Naxi pilot flying all around,
    But if one Nazi pilot should crash into the ground,
    There'd be *no* Nazi pilots flying all around.

[*Curtain*]

Classjack

CHARACTERS

CLASS 2C

ALISTAIR	ABIGAIL
BARNEY	ALISON
CHRIS	BERNADETTE
CLIVE	BEVERLEY
COLIN	EMMA
GLYN	LOUISE
IAN	MARY
JONATHAN	MICHELLE
PAUL	POLLY
TOM	STACEY ⎱ *Twins*
WILLIAM	TRACEY ⎰
WINSTON	TERESA
	WENDY

MR BENSTEAD *their teacher*

Off-Stage Voices
HEADMASTER
GIRL

The events of the play take place in a town-centre school classroom one Monday morning.

Note on Staging
Take care not to clog up your stage with furniture: use as few light tables as possible. Stools or light benches take up less space than chairs; if you're not using rostra to make the children at the back more visible try using tall stools upstage and low benches downstage. And why not put the smaller kids, including PAUL, at the front and the taller ones such as CHRIS and CLIVE at the back?

Scene 1

*A classroom, Monday morning. A door at one side leads via a corridor to
the main school. At the other side is another door leading to a stockroom.
The walls are covered with colourful and unusual displays and posters of
many kinds, including ones for Oxfam, Save the Children and similar
charities. One poster features the Bevvy Boys, a pop group. There are
masks on the wall, at least two of which are wearable. A sign behind the
teacher's desk says 'You Don't Have To Be Crazy To Teach Here But It
Helps'. Someone has crossed out 'Here' and substituted '2C'. The teacher's
desk is near the stockroom door. Behind the desk is a blackboard on which is
drawn a drummer. Underneath it says 'Good luck benny on sunday'. There
are enough seats for all the class, mostly still on the tables where the cleaners
left them on Friday. Bags, baskets and coats are strewn around. The
windows are in the fourth wall, facing the audience.*

*When the curtain rises the stockroom door is closed and the main door is
open. Through it, the distant voices of* CHILDREN *are heard singing a
song. Then the* HEADMASTER *is heard asking questions; twice the*
CHILDREN *chorus 'No, sir' in a bored sing-song. There is a bang and an
exclamation from the stockroom. The door slowly opens and* CLIVE *peers
in. He shuts the door, looks round the room, opens the teacher's desk and
pockets something before sneaking out through the main door, which he
leaves open. The* HEADMASTER *is still speaking. He asks a question.*
ALL *chorus 'No, sir'. There is a pause, then running feet are heard and*
GLYN *and* IAN *hurry in.*

GLYN: That Headmaster! Every Monday morning! He drives me
up the wall!

IAN: Same here. (*Imitating the voice we have just heard*) 'Remember
the three P's, children! What are they?'

BOTH (*sing-song*): 'Politeness, Peacefulness and Punctuality.'

> BOTH *blow a raspberry towards the door. Enter* ABIGAIL *and*
> ALISON.

ABIGAIL: Charming! What's up with you two?

IAN ⎫
GLYN ⎬ (*mocking*): 'Politeness, Peacefulness and Punctuality!'

ALISON: What's wrong with that? You should be punctual.

There is a yell from the corridor. Enter PAUL, *a small boy, frogmarched by* BARNEY.

PAUL: Gerroff! I'll tell Benny!

The rest of the CLASS *enter, except* CLIVE.

GIRLS: Leave him!

EMMA: You wait, Barney. Mr Benstead'll get you when he comes.

BARNEY: Yes, when. He wasn't in Assembly, was he?

ABIGAIL: He's late again. He's worse than Clive.

Enter CLIVE.

BEVERLEY: Talk of the devil! You just come?

CLIVE: 'Course I have.

BEVERLEY: Have you seen Mr Benstead?

CLIVE: Nah. (*He sits.*)

LOUISE: Did Benny's group have a gig at the weekend?

MICHELLE: Yes, Scotland last night. He told us on Friday that he'd be late.

IAN: Scotland! Och aye the noo!

GLYN: Hey, I bet he comes in a kilt!

BERNADETTE: Are you sure he said Scotland?

WILLIAM: It's snowing in Scotland.

MICHELLE: It says on this poster: 'April 16th: The Bevvy Boys at the Bonny Prince Charlie Motel, Glen Gloy, Perthshire.'

WINSTON: Glen Gloy! He'll be stuck there, man.

POLLY: I wonder what he'll bring us this time?

GLYN: Bagpipes.

MARY: Kippers.

TWINS: Haggis.

COLIN: Whisky.

ALL: Whisky!

ABIGAIL: I don't know what the Headmaster'll say if he brings whisky and we all get drunk. Remember when he brought all that clotted cream from Devon?

ALL (*smiling*): Yeah!

TOM: I don't like whisky. I hope he brings us a big tin of butterscotch.

CHRIS: No! Scottish football scarves!

WENDY: Yeah! Scotland! Scotland!

SOME *join in the chant,* OTHERS *start chanting 'England!'* *while* BERNADETTE, TERESA *and the* TWINS *chant 'Ireland!'* *The noise rises until* JONATHAN *goes to the teacher's desk, takes out a whistle and blows it.*

GLYN: Half time!

JONATHAN: All shut up! We don't want the Headmaster to hear us: let's work on our own.

CLIVE: You going to make us?

JONATHAN: Well, keep quiet at any rate, or he'll send Mrs Gobbet to teach us like he did last week.

ALL: Old Ma Gobbet! Ugh!

ALL *arrange the tables and seats, chatting as they do so.* ABIGAIL *and* ALISON *bring folders from the stockroom and distribute them. The* CLASS *settle down to work quietly,* SOME *muttering,* OTHERS *fetching materials from the stockroom or the desk. They are clearly used to working on their own.*

EMMA (*standing*): Register!

COLIN: That's Benny's job: let him do it.

EMMA: He's not here, is he? So we'll have to do it.

ABIGAIL: I'm the orderly: leave it to me. (*Going to the desk and opening the register*) Alistair!

ALISTAIR: What?

ABIGAIL: Are you here?

ALISTAIR: 'Course I'm here: can't you see me?

ABIGAIL: You have to say 'Here!'.

ALISTAIR: I don't have to say anything to you, Ratface.

ABIGAIL: I heard that!

ALISTAIR: Good: it shows you're not deaf as well as blind.

ABIGAIL (*marking the register*): Alistair, here. Barney. Barney!

BARNEY: What?

ABIGAIL: Are you here?

BARNEY: Yes: are you there?

EMMA: Oh, for crying out loud, just fill it in Abby!

ABIGAIL: No: perhaps they're not all here.

EMMA *blows the whistle.*

GLYN: Ninety minutes up.
EMMA: Shut up, you. Is anybody away?

ALL *look round.*

JONATHAN: Andy, Woodsy, Patsy, Reaney.
EMMA: Anybody else?
ALISON: Annie.
WINSTON: One more.
EMMA: Who?
WINSTON: Benny.
ALL: Aw, funny!
EMMA: Right, carry on. (*She marks the register.*) 25 present 5 absent. Take this to the office.
ABIGAIL: No, because the teacher has to initial it.
EMMA: Right, I'll initial it for him. *She initials it.*) F.A.B. Frederick Arthur Benstead. (*She closes the register.*) Hey, there's a letter clipped to it.
BEVERLEY: Who for?
EMMA: Mr Benstead. It says 'Personal'.
STACEY: Love letter.
TRACEY: Fan mail.
EMMA: It could be important. Shall I open it?
MARY: Ooh, no: don't!
EMMA (*holding the letter to the light*): It's from the Headmaster.

ALL *groan.*

CHRIS: What's he sending him a letter for, when he can talk to him?
BERNADETTE: 'Cause he doesn't talk to ordinary teachers.
BARNEY: 'Cause he doesn't like Benny. Or us. That's why he put us in this classroom out on our own.
BEVERLEY: Perhaps he's telling him not to bring his billygoat to school again.

Laughter.

EMMA: Shall I open it?

A mingled chorus of 'Yes' and 'No'.

ALISON: No, it's private property.

ABIGAIL (*standing*): I am going to take the register and that letter back to the office and tell them that Mr Benstead is not in school.

BARNEY (*blocking the door*): You tell 'em that and you're finished in this class, kid. (*To the* OTHERS) Right?

ALL: Right!

BARNEY: You take the register, and you don't blab about Benny: right?

ABIGAIL: All right. What about the letter?

BARNEY (*taking it*): We'll deal with this. Move!

Exit ABIGAIL.

BARNEY (*to* ALISTAIR): Here, read it.

ALISTAIR (*opening the letter and reading it*): 'Dear Mr Benstead, I am returning your cheque for the replacement of my trousers which were eaten by your goat . . . .

Laughter.

. . . as you omitted to sign it. Please sign and return. I must also inform you that at yesterday's meeting of the School Governors it was decided to give you a final warning about your persistent lateness and absences. Should you be absent or late again without good reason, you will be deemed – What's that – 'deemed'? – 'You will be deemed to have failed your probationary year.'

POLLY: That means they'll give him the sack if he's late again.

BERNADETTE: And he won't be able to teach anywhere else, either.

ALL: Aw!

TERESA: Poor old Benny.

BARNEY: Is that all?

ALISTAIR: Yes. Oh, it says 'PS Your future conduct will be closely monitored.'

POLLY: That means the Headmaster's going to spy on him.

ABIGAIL hurries in looking worried.

BARNEY: What's the matter with you? You told 'em, didn't you?

ABIGAIL: No, but the Headmaster was in the office, and he asked me if Mr Benstead had come late, and I said no, and I wasn't lying, 'cause he hasn't come at all, has he? And he said 'I'll be along to check on that young man.'

TWINS: Spying on him!

EMMA: What are we going to do if the Headmaster comes?

MARY: We can't do anything.

MICHELLE: We can put a bucket over the door!

ALL: Yeah!

CLIVE: We can lock him out!

EMMA: We haven't got a key.

CLIVE: Wanna bet?

PAUL: Tie him up! Gag him!

ALL: Yeah!

BERNADETTE: Talk sense, all of you! The first minute this Headmaster fellow sets foot in this room and sees there's no teacher here, then our Mr Benstead is for the high jump, and there is nothing that you or me or anybody else can do about it.

POLLY: Anyway, what's it matter to us if he's sacked?

LOUISE: How would you like to be out of work?

POLLY: I don't care: he's a nutter. Anyway, he has another job: playing the drums with these Bevvy Boys.

BERNADETTE: That's not a living.

TOM: I like him. He's not old, like a lot of the teachers.

GLYN: Yes, he's a good teacher.

ABIGAIL: How can he be? He's not here to teach us.

TOM: But when he is here he's brilliant.

IAN: Yes, he's good fun.

POLLY: He's not supposed to be funny: he's supposed to teach us things.

BEVERLEY: Well, he does, doesn't he?

ALISON: I think he should be more strict, like Mr Orchard.

ALL *groan at the thought of the dreaded Mr Orchard.*

IAN (*standing and imitating a stern teacher*): Another sound from any of you and you will be punished severely: tortured by Orchard!

Laughter.

MARY: I like Mrs Webb.

POLLY: Yes, 'cause you're one or her favourites.

WENDY: Yes, Webby's not a good teacher: she either loves you or hates you. Good teachers don't have favourites.

WINSTON: The trouble with Benny is he likes everybody, even Chris.

CHRIS: What's that supposed to mean?

WILLIAM: I say that Benny's the best teacher we have. He's fair, you can have a laugh with him, he makes things interesting, and he can be strict when he wants.

BERNADETTE: Right. And if Benny gets the sack we'll have old Ma Gobbet teaching us, and we all know what she's like. She's lethal.

ALL (*gloomily*): Yeah.

LOUISE: But we're only kids: we can't do anything. Either Benny comes or he doesn't. And if the Head finds out he's not here he'll sack him.

BEVERLEY (*looking out above the audience*): Somebody behind the bikesheds. Perhaps it's Benny going to park his bike.

ALL look out.

WENDY: It's only the caretaker.

There is a loud knock on the door. ALL freeze. The knocking is repeated, louder.

GIRL (*off*): Mr Benstead!

TOM (*calling*): Mr Benstead's not here!

ALL stare at TOM in exasperation.

GIRL (*off*): Well, where is he then?

JONATHAN (*standing*): He's . . . He's in his back room.

GIRL (*off*): Well, tell him he has to see the Headmaster in his office.

JONATHAN: When?

GIRL (*off*):Now.

JONATHAN: No, wait a minute!

JONATHAN goes to the door and opens it.

JONATHAN: She's gone.

STACEY (*to* TOM): Why did you say he wasn't here?

TOM: Well, I didn't think, did I?

TWINS: No, you never do, do you?

ABIGAIL: I bet the Headmaster comes himself next time.

ALL: Yeah.

MICHELLE: And we still haven't thought of anything to say to him if he comes.

PAUL: We'll tell him that Benny has just slipped out to the shop for something he forgot.

ALL *groan*.

ALISTAIR: How about this? We all slip out into town, and leave a note from Benny saying he's taken us out to do a survey of the shops.

ALL *look at each other and nod*.

ALL: All right.

MICHELLE: I'll write it up on the board. Here.

MICHELLE *writes on the board in large letters: 'Dear Sir, We have gone into town to do a survay of the shop's with mr Benstead. True. Your's sincerly 2C'. She then adds three kisses.*

BEVERLEY: Don't put kisses! Who wants to kiss a Headmaster?

MICHELLE *shrugs and rubs out the kisses.*

CLIVE: Right: let's climb out of the back window!

BERNADETTE: No, the caretaker'll tell on us. We'll have to sneak down the corridor.

BERNADETTE *goes to the door, opens it and slams it shut.*

BERNADETTE: Headmaster's coming!

BARNEY: Clive! Lock the door!

CLIVE *takes a key from his pocket and locks the door. The* OTHERS *stare.*

MARY: Where did you get that key?

There is a knock on the door. ALL freeze. Someone tries the door.

HEADMASTER (*off*): Mr Benstead! Mr Benstead! Are you there?
Why is this door locked? (*Silence*) Children, this is your
Headmaster speaking! Are you there?
PAUL (*standing*): Yes, we're here sir.

*ALL turn to PAUL in silent fury, mouthing insults. PAUL puts
his hand to his mouth as he realises what he has done.*

CLIVE (*whispering*): You stupid dimwit!
HEADMASTER (*off*): Is Mr Benstead with you, children?

ALL look at each other in panic, dismay or despair.

HEADMASTER (*off, thumping on the door*): For the last time! Are
you there, Mr Benstead?
ALISTAIR (*standing*): Yes, he is here. Mr Headmaster, sir!

ALL stare at ALISTAIR.

EMMA (*whispering*): What did you say that for?
HEADMASTER (*off*): Oh. Good. Well, if he's there, why does he
not answer me?
ALISTAIR: Because . . . Because he is tied up, sir. And gagged.
HEADMASTER (*off*): *What* did you say?
ALISTAIR: He's bound and gagged, sir. On the floor. In the
stockroom.

*SOME of the class start to giggle, and put their hands to their
mouths to stop themselves laughing. As the conversation continues, the
whole class except ALISTAIR are laughing silently, SOME swaying
helplessly, SOME even rolling on the floor. The door handle rattles
again.*

HEADMASTER (*off*): Why have you tied up your teacher, 2C?
Untie him at once or I shall report the matter to the proper
authorities.
MARY: We didn't tie him up, sir: we like him.
HEADMASTER (*off*): Then who did tie him up? And why have
you not released him?

ALISTAIR *is running out of ideas, but the* OTHERS *help him by miming or whispering.*

ALISTAIR: Sir, we are in the fingers . . . in the *hands* of two tall . . . *high* . . . *hi-jackers*, sir. They . . . sounds like pumped . . . *jumped* through the window and tied up Mr Benstead. They have guns, and bombs and masks. They want money or they will kill us all, one by one.

HEADMASTER (*off*): Good heavens! This is most alarming! May I talk to them?

ALISTAIR: I am afraid not: they do not speak good English, sir. But they say Mr Benstead is brave. He fought like a cat . . . a lion! They will write you a ransom note. Now go away or they will shoot us one by one. They are waving their guns about. And do not tell the police. Understand?

HEADMASTER (*off*): Yes, I understand.

ALISTAIR: Then return to your room and wait for the note. Quickly! They are aiming their guns at the door!

COLIN (*looking through the keyhole*): He's running down the corridor like mad! He's gone!

ALL *explode into laughter.*

BEVERLEY: He believed you!

ALISTAIR: I'm just a genius, kid.

IAN (*imitating the* HEADMASTER): Why have you tied him up? I shall report the matter to the, er . . .

ALL: The proper authorities!

IAN: The proper authorities.

BARNEY: We've beaten the Headmaster! We are the champions!

SOME *join in, but the* OTHERS *shush them.*

BARNEY: Why should we be quiet?

TERESA: 'Cause we've just told him we've been hi-jacked.

WENDY: And these hi-jackers aren't going to let us chant and yell, are they?

CHRIS: What hi-jackers? There aren't any.

TERESA: But the Headmaster doesn't know that, does he? We've got to act as if there were hi-jackers here.

LOUISE: Yes, and we'd better write that letter fast.

COLIN: What letter?

LOUISE: The ransom note from the hi-jackers asking for money or they'll shoot us all, one by one.

>   MARY *bursts into hysterical weeping.*

JONATHAN: What's the matter now?

MARY: I don't want to be shot one by one!

>   ALL *groan.*

EMMA: Shush, Mary: you'll be all right.

GLYN: Let's get this letter written.

JONATHAN: Okay. Get a pen and paper.

ALISON: I've got a notepad, and a pen.

JONATHAN: Ta. (*He looks at the pad.*) Oh, no! We can't write a ransom note on this!

ALISON: I got it for my birthday! It's nice!

JONATHAN: Yes, and it's pink and it's got flowers and soppy poetry on it. Listen:

>   (*reading*) 'I don't need money to make me content,
>
>   I am not by riches beguiled.'

ALL (*disgusted*): Beguiled!

JONATHAN (*reading*): 'But the birds and the flowers

>   And the sunlit hours
>
>   And the smile in the heart of a child.'

ALL (*mocking*): Aw!

JONATHAN (*scornful*): 'I don't need money'! Give me some more paper, somebody.

GLYN (*tearing out a sheet of paper*): Here.

JONATHAN (*looking at it*): You joking? This is worse!

GLYN: Why? It hasn't got flowers on it.

JOHNATHAN (*pointing*): What's it say, there?

GLYN: I can't read my own writing. Oh, yes. 'Our Headmaster look like Draclia.'

WINSTON: It's *Dracula*, man not 'Draclia'. Change it to 'He looks like Dracula'.

BERNADETTE: You can't put that either.

GLYN: Why not?

BERNADETTE: Because he doesn't look like Dracula, does he? He looks more like Frankenstein.

TWINS: Or a monster from outer space.

ALL: Yeah!

WILLIAM: That's good: put that.

JONATHAN: He's not going to collect money for us if we call him names, is he? (*Silence*) Is he?

ALL (*reluctantly*): No.

JONATHAN: Right. Give me some plain paper.

ABIGAIL *tears a sheet from a pad and gives it to him.*

BEVERLEY: Let Tom write it.

TOM: Aw, why me?

BEVERLEY: 'Cause these hi-jackers are supposed to be foreigners, so they wouldn't write well, would they?

TOM: All right. (*Writing*) 'Dear Sir, We have tied up the teacher . . . '

JONATHAN: You don't spell 'teacher' like that.

TOM: Yes, I do. (*Writing*) 'And we are keeping the little ones as . . . (*He writes silently, mouthing the words.*)

JONATHAN: Look what you've put! Tell 'em how you've spelled 'hostages.'

TOM: O-S-T-R-I-C-H-E-S.

Laughter.

BEVERLEY: That spells 'Ostriches'. It should be 'hostages'. H-O-S-T-A-G-E-S.

TOM: Oh, all right. (*He alters it, spelling as he does so.*) We are keeping the little ones as hostages until you give us . . . How much money shall I ask for?

WENDY: Why are you asking for money?

TOM: That's what kidnappers do: they ask for money.

MICHELLE: Hi-jackers don't: they ask for prisoners to be released.

LOUISE: The Headmaster hasn't got any prisoners.

IAN: I bet he has, locked up in his study.

LOUISE: Talk sense. Just say they'll kill us one by one unless the Headmaster pays us lots of money.

ALL: Yeah!

ALISTAIR: You can't just put 'lots'.

TOM: How much shall I ask for?

PAUL: I'd say about ninety nine pounds.

ALL (*scornful*): Ninety nine!

TWINS: Why not a hundred?

PAUL: We don't want to push our luck, do we?

BARNEY: A hundred's not enough for all of us. I say ask for masses of money.

ALL: Yeah!

WENDY: A million!

CHRIS: Two million!

LOUISE: Five million!

WILLIAM: Ten million!

TERESA: A hundred million!

PAUL: And a tube of Smarties each.

TOM: All right. Shall I put that – A hundred million pounds and a tube of Smarties each?

PAUL: Yes. A hundred million pounds and a *big* tube of Smarties each.

ALL: A hundred million pounds and a *big* tube of Smarties each, yeah!

Silence. ALL smile, thinking about the money.

MARY (*raising a hand*): I think it should be a bit less.

PAUL: Yes. Just the tube of Smarties.

ALL: No!

WINSTON: We've got to be realistic, man. Ask for £10,000 each, okay?

ALL: Okay.

TOM (*writing*): We want £10,000 each . . .

WINSTON: Don't put that, man! How many of us are there?

ABIGAIL: Twenty-five.

WINSTON: Right. So ask for £25,000, then.

JONATHAN: Twenty-five times £10,000 is £250,000. That's a quarter of a million.

ALL: A quarter of a million!

JONATHAN: Write that down: two hundred and fifty thousand pounds.

TOM: How many noughts?

JONATHAN: Four.

PAUL: And twenty five tubes of Smarties.

POLLY: Hey, I saw this film and these kidnappers left a note in a tin in a wall and it said 'Do not tell the police or it will be the worse for your kids.'

TOM: Say it slower.

> POLLY *repeats it while* TOM *writes it.*

COLIN: Then you put 'Yours truthfully.'

MARY: No, put 'Love from the hi-jackers.'

All (*scornful*): Love!

ABIGAIL: Put 'Yours sincerely' like on the board.

TOM (*writing*): 'Yours sincerely.' How shall I sign it?

PAUL: Put your name: Tom Seymour.

ALL: No!

TOM: I'll just put 'Yours sincerely, The hi-jackers.'

ALL: Right.

> TOM *finishes writing and folds the letter.*

TERESA: Who's going to deliver it?

> *Silence.*

PAUL: Not me.

GLYN: The Headmaster could capture the messenger and make 'em tell the truth.

ALL: Yeah.

POLLY: Or we could leave it in a tin in a wall.

BEVERLEY: I know! We'll put it in a tin, like Polly says, and throw it right down the corridor. Somebody's forced to find it.

WENDY: No. Some teacher'll think it's litter and put it in a waste basket.

ALL: Mmm.

MICHELLE: There's only one way: somebody'll have to run down the corridor and throw it into the Head's office and run back before he can catch 'em.

ALISON; Right, who's the fastest runner?

ALL: Paul!

PAUL: Aw, no!

MICHELLE: Aw, yes! Here, grab this tin. (*She puts the letter in.*) Clive'll unlock the door and you scoot down the corridor, sling the tin into the Head's office and rush back here. Right?

PAUL: Can I go to the loo while I'm out?

ALL: No!

MICHELLE: Do as you're told. Unlock the door, Clive. Anybody in the corridor?

CLIVE: No, it's empty.

MICHELLE: It's fifty yards, that's six seconds each way and one second to the throw the tin. Thirteen seconds. We'll all count.

BARNEY: And if you're not back in thirteen seconds, I'll come and get you, kid. Right?

PAUL: Right.

MICHELLE: Open the door. On your marks. Get set. Go!

PAUL *runs out.* ALL *count to thirteen. They stare at the doorway.*

BARNEY: The little rat.

LOUISE: I bet the Headmaster's captured him and found out everything and Benny'll be sacked.

ALISTAIR: He's coming back!

PAUL *runs back in.* CLIVE *locks the door.*

BARNEY: Did you throw the tin into his room?

PAUL (*doing a thumbs-up sign*): Yup!

ALL *cheer.*

BARNEY: The Headmaster's sitting there scared to death 'cause he thinks we're being threatened by armed hi-jackers, and he thinks if he doesn't pay the money they'll shoot us and it'll be on the news and everybody'll think this is a bad school and he'll get the sack. So he'll *have* to pay!

ALL: Yeah!

TOM: It's a good letter.

ALL: Yeah.

PAUL (*producing the letter*): Yes, it is.

> ALL *stare at the letter*.

WILLIAM: What's that?

PAUL: It's our letter.

BARNEY: You said you threw it into the Head's room!

PAUL: No, the tin. Michelle said throw the tin. That's why I took longer, 'cause I had to get the letter out of the tin before I threw it.

> ALL *groan in exasperation*.

BARNEY: Give me another tin, quick. (*Putting the letter in*) Right: this time you leave the letter in the tin, and you throw this tin with the letter inside it into the Head's room. Right?

PAUL: Do I have to?

ALL: Yes!!

PAUL: Oh, all right.

> CLIVE *unlocks the door*.

ALL: On your marks! Get set! Go!

> CLIVE *opens the door*, PAUL *scampers out and* ALL *start counting again. At 'ten'* PAUL *races back in and sits panting*. CLIVE *locks the door*.

EMMA: Was he there?

PAUL: Yes, I threw it right at him.

> ALL *cheer*.

TERESA: So all we have to do now is wait.

TWINS: What's all this money for?

WINSTON: What do you mean, chickies, 'What's it for?'?

TWINS: What are we going to do with it?

WINSTON: We're going to spend it! I'm going to buy me a Porsche!

WILLIAM: I'm going to buy a helicopter. A chopper.

BERNADETTE: I'm going to buy a home entertainment centre with everything.

Just Like Us

LOUISE: I'm going to go ice-skating every day.

TWINS: Hi-jackers don't ask for money for themselves: they do it for a group.

BERNADETTE: What, like a pop-group?

TRACEY: No! Like the Palestine Liberation Movement.

STACEY: They want to free things, like free Palestine.

PAUL: Free range eggs.

IAN: Free bears and Goldilocks.

Laughter

TWINS: Don't be silly.

TRACEY: Hi-jackers use the money to *save* things.

ABIGAIL: Oh, right, like Save Wildlife.

POLLY: Save the Children.

LOUISE: Save the Whale.

PAUL: Save milk-bottle tops.

TERESA: Save Mr Benstead.

ALL: Yeah: Save Mr Benstead!

BARNEY: But he doesn't need the money: he has enough. I say it's our money, all of it.

WILLIAM: Well, what I want to know is: when we get it, where are we going to put it?

WENDY: Stockroom.

WILLIAM: But what's Mr Benstead going to say when he finds millions of pounds in his stockroom?

TOM: Perhaps he won't notice it.

ALISON: That policeman last week said not to leave money lying around where it might get stolen.

ABIGAIL: Yes, he said ask for a cheque, then put it in the bank.

TERESA: How can we? We don't have a bank account! We can't say 'Make all cheques and postal orders payable to the Save Mr Benstead Fund' can we?

Pause.

ALISTAIR: No, it'll have to be cash: we'll ask for used £10 and £5 notes.

BEVERLEY: Yes, and split it between us. £10,000 each.

MARY: Oh, what's my Mum going to say when I bring all this

money home? She'll kill me for stealing.

LOUISE: Keep it in your room.

MARY: I sleep with my sisters. They'll take it.

BARNEY: I'll keep it for you, kid.

MARY: You won't. I don't want it.

TWINS: We don't either.

BARNEY: What?

TWINS: We don't want it.

TRACEY: Money doesn't bring happiness.

BARNEY: All right, you don't have to take it. Hands up if you want £10,000!

Hesitation. ALL look at each other, then SOME start raising their hands.

CHRIS: Me.

MICHELLE: Yes, I do.

EMMA: I'd like £10,000.

ABIGAIL: Ooh, Emma, it's wrong.

EMMA: Why? We can give it to charity if we want. Like the Third World. Or the Cats' Protection League.

BARNEY: Make your minds up. Hands up if you want £10,000.

MOST of the class raise their hands.

BARNEY: Who doesn't want it? Hands up! Others, hands down.

A FEW raise their hands, including, ABIGAIL, ALISON, the TWINS, MARY, PAUL and TOM.

COLIN (*to* TOM): I thought you wanted it.

TOM: No, it's too much. I only want a hundred.

BARNEY: Put your hand down and give me the extra £9,900.

TOM (*lowering his hand*): Okay.

CHRIS (*to* MARY): And give me yours, or else!

GLYN: Shut it! Leave her alone! We'll share what people don't want between Mr Benstead and charities.

There is a knock at the door. ALL freeze and look at the door. An envelope is pushed underneath. ABIGAIL picks it up.

JONATHAN: What's it say?

ABIGAIL: 'To the Hi-jackers.' Shall I open it? Perhaps it's the money!

ALL: Yes!

ABIGAIL *opens the envelope and looks at the letter.*

BARNEY: Who's it from? The Headmaster? (ABIGAIL *nods.*)

CHRIS: What's it say? Do we get the money?

ABIGAIL *gives the letter to* JONATHAN.

WENDY: Where's the money?

MICHELLE: Read it, Johnny.

JONATHAN (*reading*): 'Dear Sirs, Thank you for your letter. I have not informed the police about the hi-jacking. However, I regret to say that your demand for £250,000 and 25 tubes of Smarties is exorbitant.'

LOUISE: What's that mean?

MICHELLE: Too much.

JONATHAN (*reading*): 'The school Tuckshop Fund contains £349 and there is £175 in the PTA Fund, a grand total of £524. I have asked the bank to send the money. Please do not harm Class 2C, as they are very precious to all of us.'

Laughter.

JONATHAN (*reading*): 'PS We only have 19 tubes of Smarties in the Tuckshop.' And that's it, signed with all his letters after his name.

CHRIS: Five hundred and twenty four quid between all of us! How much is that each?

MICHELLE: About twenty one pounds.

TERESA: Twenty one pounds! I've never had so much!

WENDY: Twenty one's nothing.

JONATHAN: We asked for a quarter of a million: what do we do?

COLIN: I say hold out for it or start killing people. Well, pretend to.

TERESA: I say, take what he's offering.

COLIN: Let's vote on it.

There is a knock on the door. ALL *look at the door. The knock is repeated.*

JONATHAN: Hello? Who is it?

HEADMASTER (*off*): It's me, the Headmaster.

CLIVE: What do you want?

HEADMASTER (*off*): I've brought the money.

TOM *begins to cheer.* BARNEY *puts a hand over his mouth.*

JONATHAN: Good. Push it under the door.

HEADMASTER (*off*): I can't: the envelope's too thick.

EMMA: Open the door!

CHRIS: Don't! It might be a trap! They'll rush in, like the SAS.

BEVERLEY: How are we going to get the money, then?

POLLY: I bet there isn't any. (*Calling*) You haven't brought any money, have you? You're always lying, you!

WENDY: Yes! You said we could have a new classroom this year, but we haven't, have we?

ALL: No!

BEVERLEY: And you said we could have a separate Christmas party from the first forms, but we didn't, did we?

ALL: No!

GLYN: And you promised we could watch the football when it rained, but we didn't!

HEADMASTER (*off*): Stop insulting me! Who is in charge there? I demand to talk to the hi-jackers! Why do they remain silent? Are they still there?

Silence. ALL *look at each other, then at* IAN, *pointing to the door.* IAN *goes to the door, takes a breath, getting into the role of hi-jacker. Then he speaks in a strong foreign accent.*

IAN: Who are you, you noisy person?

HEADMASTER (*off*): I am the Headmaster of this school, Mr Gussett. Are you a hi-jacker?

IAN: Of course I am. We have remained silent because we wish to remain silent. I am holding a machine-gun. My friend is holding the bombs. Where is the money?

HEADMASTER (*off*): I have it here.

IAN: That is good. Are you alone?

HEADMASTER (*off*): Yes, I am. Completely alone. No-one is with me. Not anybody, I assure you. Open the door.

TWINS (*near the door*): Don't open it! Somebody's whispering!

TRACEY (*looking through the keyhole*): There's a whole gang of 'em.

IAN (*calling, still as hi-jacker*): We do not trust you! Put the money on the floor. I shall count to five, and if you are still there we shall blow up your little ones with a big bomb. One, two, three, four, five!

TRACEY: They've all gone.

JONATHAN: Open the door.

> CLIVE *unlocks the door, picks up the packet which is lying outside and re-locks the door.*

EMMA: Twenty pounds each! Open it!

CLIVE (*opening the packet*): There's another packet inside. And a letter.

MICHELLE: We can play Pass the Parcel.

EMMA: Give me the packet, quick!

> MICHELLE *takes the letter, and* CLIVE *passes the packet to* EMMA, *who opens it and throws the contents in the air with a shout.* ALL *except for* MICHELLE *scramble excitedly for the paper that flutters down, then stand silent, staring at the rectangles of paper in their hands.*

WENDY: Just bits of newspaper!

MICHELLE (*reading the letter*): 'Dear Hi-jackers, I have discussed your demand for money with my senior staff, and we have decided that we cannot yield to your threats.'

ALL: Aw!

MICHELLE: 'Firstly, if we give you money, we are encouraging you to kidnap other innocent children. Secondly, we do not know whether you will keep your promise to release the children. Thirdly, the money is urgently needed for a new drinks dispenser in the staffroom. Lastly, to be quite honest, none of us cares very much what happens to Class 2C, or their teacher.'

ALL: Aw!

WENDY: A drinks dispenser!

MICHELLE: Shush! 'I enclose one tube of Smarties. PS Please do not shoot the kiddies, as it will look bad in the papers. But if you do shoot them, please avoid getting blood on the floor, as this will annoy the cleaning staff and give them extra work. Yours sincerely, G.F. Gussett, B.Econ, FRSO, GW, RSVP, Headmaster.

PPS Rest assured that I shall not call the police.' That's it.

Silence.

TOM: Where's the Smarties?

MICHELLE (*looking in the envelope*): Here.

TOM: Brilliant! Give us one!

JONATHAN: Share 'em out.

MICHELLE *shares them out. They eat them.*

WILLIAM: Tell you what.

ALL: What?

WILLIAM: I'm still hungry.

ALL *groan.*

JONATHAN: What time is it?

ALISTAIR: Nearly break-time.

Silence.

ABIGAIL: I don't think Mr Benstead's coming today.

ALISON: No. We've given him a chance and he hasn't taken it.

MICHELLE: So what do we do now? Tell the Headmaster that we've been fooling him all morning?

ABIGAIL: What else can we do?

TERESA: Just stay here. Pretend we're still being hi-jacked.

ALISON: And what happens at the end of the day? The longer we stay, the worse it'll be for us.

COLIN: I say shoot somebody and say we'll kill the others if they don't give us the money.

WINSTON: Oh, come on, man, we can't just sit around shooting each other.

COLIN: Why? Why not? Why can't we? Go on, tell me!

WINSTON: 'Cause we got no guns, man.

COLIN: Oh, right. (*He thinks.*) I've got a penknife. (*He produces a tiny knife.*)

WILLIAM: Oh, brilliant: I can just see us chopping each other to bits with that. Take a week.

LOUISE: If I don't get my dinner I'll starve to death.

MARY: My Mum'll kill me if I die of starvation! I'm a growing girl!

WENDY: Yes, growing more stupid every minute.

JONATHAN: Shut up! Nobody's going to starve!

COLIN (*looking out of the window above the audience*): Here they come!

ALL: Who?

COLIN: Two policemen. One's hiding behind the coke store and one's just dodged behind that wall there.

ABIGAIL: And the Headmaster promised not to tell the police!

ALL: Yeah!

TWINS: Big cheat!

BERNADETTE: We can't let him win now!

   A bell rings.

WENDY: Five minutes to break, then I'm going to eat. Who else is coming?

MARY ⎫
LOUISE ⎭ : Me.

EMMA: You'll spoil everything! You can't go!

WENDY ⎫
MARY ⎬ : Wanna bet?
LOUISE ⎭

COLIN (*still looking out of the window*): Benny's coming!

ALL (*looking out*): Where?

COLIN: Over there: on his bike, stopped at the lights. See him?

ALL: Yes!

BERNADETTE: The police are still looking this way.

BEVERLEY: Benny'll put his bike in the shed and climb through the stockroom window like he always does.

COLIN: No. Police'll stop him and the Head'll know everything. Lights've changed. He's coming.

TERESA: What a shame.

POLLY: I said it was a waste of time.

CHRIS (*who has been whispering to* CLIVE): Give us two masks, quick!

JONATHAN (*handing him the masks*): What for?

COLIN: He's wheeling his bike through the side gate.

CLIVE: Alistair said that these hi-jackers wore masks, right? Chris and me'll put these masks on and climb out of the back window and the police'll think we're the hi-jackers and chase us.

MARY: They'll catch you.

CHRIS: No way. We'll shin over the bakery wall and chuck the masks away and they won't know it's us. Then we'll sneak back.

CLIVE: Put 'em on, quick!

> CHRIS *and* CLIVE *don the masks.*

COLIN: He's putting his bike away. They haven't seen him.

CLIVE: Move it, Chris! Go, go, go!

ALISON: Wait!

CHRIS ⎫
CLIVE ⎭ : We can't. See you!

> CHRIS *and* CLIVE, *wearing the masks, hurry into the stockroom.*

WILLIAM (*looking out*): Benny's gone back: he's forgotten something.

TOM: Presents!

WILLIAM: Police are still looking this way. Hey! Chris and Clive are racing across the yard! Police've seen 'em!

BEVERLEY: They're chasing 'em! The kids are climbing the wall!

BERNADETTE: They're running along the wall! The police can't follow 'em! They've gone!

WILLIAM: Benny's coming out of the bike shed again.

ABIGAIL: All look as if we're working!

> ALL *sit and look studious. The stockroom door slowly opens and* MR BENSTEAD *enters. He stands smiling at the* CLASS.

MR BENSTEAD: Hi, kids!

CLASS (*not looking up*): Hi, sir!

MR BENSTEAD: You're all very quiet. Something wrong?

CLASS: No, sir.

TOM: Have you brought us a present, sir, please?

MR BENSTEAD: Don't I always? Here you are: catch!

TOM: Butterscotch! Great!

> Mr BENSTEAD *throws the butterscotch sweets to the* CLASS, *who scramble for them, thanking him. They sit, grinning.*

MR BENSTEAD: Did you miss me, Winston?

WINSTON: Never noticed you weren't here, Benny boy.

> *Laughter.*

BERNADETTE: Did you have a good gig, sir, in Scotland?

MR BENSTEAD: What gig? I just overslept, didn't I?

GLYN: Come off it, sir: how did it go?

MR BENSTEAD: Brilliant. They made us play an extra set, and there was a great party afterwards with lots of reporters. I wish you could all have been there.

MICHELLE: Yes, it's been pretty boring here without you, hasn't it, kids?

CLASS (*smiling*): Yeah!

MR BENSTEAD: Have you taken the register, Abby?

ABIGAIL: Yes, sir. Five absent.

MR BENSTEAD (*looking round*): I count seven missing.

> *Silence. The* CLASS *look at each other.*

BARNEY: It's Chris and Clive, sir: they just went out for a minute. Didn't they, kids?

ALL (*smiling*): Yeah.

MR BENSTEAD: Hmm. Get on with your work.

> ALL *work quietly, smiling.* MR BENSTEAD *picks up the letter from the Headmaster.*

MR BENSTEAD (*reading*): 'Dear Hi-jackers'. What's this?

JONATHAN (*snatching the letter*): It's a game, sir, called Classjack, about this class of kids who get hi-jacked in their classroom for a quarter of a million pounds.

MR BENSTEAD (*looking round at the smiling faces*): You're conning me, aren't you? Now, what have you all been up to? Come on!

Silence. There is a knock at the door.

MR BENSTEAD: Come in! (*Pause*) Come in!

COLIN: It's locked, sir.

MR BENSTEAD: Why is it locked? (*Looking in his drawer and patting his pocket*) And where's my key?

More knocking. TRACEY *looks through the keyhole.*

TRACEY: It's the Headmaster, sir, and lots of other people, some with cameras.

More knocking.

HEADMASTER (*off*): Mr Benstead! Have they released you? We've all been so worried about you.

MR BENSTEAD: Yes, I'm here, Headmaster: nothing to worry about. I got away eventually.

HEADMASTER (*off*): There are some press photographers here. They'd like to take pictures of you and your class. We're all so proud of you!

MR BENSTEAD (*to the* CLASS): Proud of me! They must have heard about the gig last night!

BARNEY: That's right, sir: they must! Right, all gather round for the photos! Get your skates on!

Quickly the CLASS *push* MR BENSTEAD *into a chair and arrange themselves round him in a smiling group facing the door.* CHRIS *and* CLIVE *rush in from the stockroom, see what is happening and slip into the group.* CLIVE *drops the key into* MR BENSTEAD's *pocket.*

MR BENSTEAD: Big smiles! (*He puts his hand in his pocket and finds the key.*) That's funny! All sit still!

He goes to the door and unlocks it, then resumes his place. ALL *smile broadly.*

MR BENSTEAD: Come in!

The door is flung open. Cheers and applause from off-stage. ALL *continue to smile. Flashes explode as photographers take pictures. More cheers, applause and flashes.* ALL *wave and smile.*

[*Curtain*]

New World

CHARACTERS

ANTONIO	ANITA	
FRANCISCO	EVA	
JOSE	JUANITA	
JUAN	MARIA	
LUIS	NATALIA	*their girlfriends*
MANUEL	RAMONA	
PABLO	ROSA	
PEDRO	ROSALIA	

CHRISTOPHER COLUMBUS	SISTER JOSEPH,	*an older nun*
TOURISTS	SISTER MICHAEL SISTER GABRIEL	*younger nuns*

SCENE A small coastal town in Spain
TIME 1492 to the present

Note
Columbus's globe has no America or Australasia, and Europe and Asia stretch round to cover about three-quarters of the Earth's circumference, so that Japan looks quite near to Europe.

Scene 1

The square of a small coastal town in Spain. A hot day. The sound of seagulls. JOSE, MANUEL, JUAN, LUIS, PEDRO *AND* FRANCISCO *are sitting looking bored.*

JOSE: Somebody turning off the main road.
OTHERS: Oh, yeah.

    Silence.

LUIS: Why is this town so hot today?
PEDRO: No sea-breeze.
LUIS: Right. Whew! You could fry an egg on the pavement.
PEDRO: Yes. If we had an egg.
MANUEL: Or a pavement.
ALL: Mmm.
FRANCISCO: Hey! Look who it is!
ALL: Pablo!

    Enter PABLO *carrying a duffel-bag with a parrot on his shoulder.*

JOSE: Hallo, Pablo!
ALL: Hallo, Pablo!
PABLO: Hola. Hot as ever, eh? Still, not as bad as Africa.
JOSE: Just got back from Africa, Pablo?
PABLO: What's it look like? (*He sits.*)
JUAN: Who's the parrot for?
PABLO: Oh, this. It's for Rosa, if she's still my girlfriend, after two years. She still around?
JUAN: Er, yes, she's still around.
PABLO: Good. Valuable bird, this.
JUAN: What's valuable about it? Just an ordinary parrot, isn't it?
PABLO: Oh yes? Suppose I told you that I've taught it the flamenco? This is a dancing parrot.
ALL: A dancing parrot!
PEDRO: Hey, let's see it dance!
PABLO: No, it's tired.
ALL: Go on!
PABLO: No!

ALL: Go on!!

PABLO: No!!

PEDRO: I don't believe it can dance.

LUIS: Right. It looks too stupid.

MANUEL: It looks dead.

PABLO: 'Course it's not dead! Watch

He takes the parrot from his shoulder and puts it on the ground. It falls over. The OTHERS jeer.

MANUEL: See: it's dead!

PABLO: No! It's just tired out with the voyage from Africa.

ALL: It's dead!

PABLO (*picking it up*): It's not dead! It's just . . . (*he listens for its heartbeat*) It's dead. (*He cuddles it and weeps.*) It's dead!

ALL: Aw!

ANTONIO (*off*): All the latest! Read all about it!

Enter ANTONIO carrying newspapers.

ANTONIO: Latest edition! Startling stories! Read all about it!

FRANCISCO: What's come over you, Antonio?

ANTONIO: Got a job, haven't I? Selling newspapers. I'm not just sitting on my butt waiting for work like you lot. Buy a paper! Seville Observer!

JOSE: Any girls on Page 3?

Laughter.

ANTONIO: Sorry, only two pages. It's a good read, though. Come on: only one peseta. (*He offers the paper to each of the* MEN, *who ignore him.*) What's wrong? Why don't you buy a paper?

JUAN: You know why: 'cause we've no money, have we?

ANTIONIO: No.

MANUEL: And we can't read either.

ANTONIO: No. Oh, hi, Pablo!

PABLO: Hi. So how many papers have you sold?

ANTONIO: Er, none.

ALL: None!

ANTONIO: None at all: waste of time. (*He sits.*) There must be a better way of making money.

PEDRO: Not selling papers, I'll tell you that. What good's reading to us? Reading's for clerks and monks and nuns. We're real men. Working men. Aren't we?

LUIS: Yes. Working men with no work.

MANUEL: Well, we'd crew a ship if anybody asked us. Do they ask us?

ALL: No.

FRANCISCO: We'd do farm work if there was any. Is there any?

ALL: No.

JOSE: So we've no money for clothes.

JUAN: No money for drink.

FRANCISCO: No money to take the girls out.

ALL (*yearning*): Girls!

ANTONIO: You can take a girl out without money.

FRANCISCO: No, you can't, because you need money to marry her, and a girl won't go out with you unless you promise to marry her. Eva won't go out with me. Will Anita go out with you if you can't sell any papers?

ANTONIO: You know she won't.

PEDRO: You're out of luck, kid. We're all dead poor and ignorant.

PABLO: Here, I'll buy a paper if you'll read it to us. Here's my last peseta. Okay?

ANTONIO (*taking the coin*): Okay.

LUIS: Any jobs advertised?

ANTONIO (*looking in the paper*): Er, yes! (*Reading*) Librarian wanted. Fluency in Greek and Arabic desirable.

   ALL *groan*.

ANTONIO: All right. How about being a cabinet-maker or a swordsmith? Both in Seville.

JUAN: No, Seville's a long walk. Besides, you got to be apprentice-trained. Any farming jobs?

ANTONIO: Not round here.

FRANCISCO: Look under merchant seamen.

ANTONIO: No. Oh yes, here. (*Reading*) 'Could you use 1000 pesetas?'

ALL: Yeah!

ANTONIO: 'Explorer seeks adventurous men to sail West with him. See news columns for further details.'

Laughter.

PABLO: West! We all know what's to the West. Thousands of miles of Atlantic, then you fall off the edge of the world. This bloke must be mad. I'm surprised he's not advertising to fly to the moon.

Laughter.

ANTONIO: Sorry, no jobs for you, then.

MANUEL: All right. Read some of these startling stories that you were yapping on about.

ANTONIO: Oh, right. (*Looking through the paper*) Er, er, er, no, er . . . .

PABLO: What do you mean: 'Er, er, er, no, er'? Read all the news.

ANTONIO: Er . . . .

ALL: Read it!

ANTONIO: Right! Here we are! 'In the last two months, no rain has fallen in Southern Spain.'

ALL *groan.*

JOSE: That's not news! It's only news here if rain *does* fall!

ALL: Right!

ANTONIO: All right! Er, here! This is news! A man in Seville has discovered marmalade.

ALL: What?

ANTONIO: Marmalade.

MANUEL: What's that, then? New country is it?

ANTONIO: No, it's, er, it sounds like a sort of orange-flavoured jam.

ALL (*disgusted*): Ugh!

MANUEL: Orange-flavoured jam! That'll never catch on, will it?

ALL: Never.

ANTONIO: All right. A guy in Jerez has invented a new drink. He calls it sherry.

ALL: Sherry?

ANTONIO: It says here you mix white wine and brandy and leave
    it in oak barrels for several years.

LUIS: Well, nobody's going to wait that long, are they?

ALL: Nah.

ANTONIO: All right: what about this? Bloke here says the best
    way to the East is to sail West. Oh, he must be the one who
    advertised for sailors. Yes. '"Sail West to reach East" says
    explorer.'

Laughter.

PEDRO: Oh, yes. And you can run fast by standing still and my
    father's my mother and pigs can fly.

PABLO: This paper of yours is all about nutters. I want my money
    back.

ANTONIO: That's not fair: you've read it!

PABLO: Life's not fair. Give me my peseta back!

ANTONIO: No way! You've had your money's worth.

PABLO: No, you read it, I didn't. Give!

The OTHERS *shout support as the two push each other. A
handbell is heard.*

JOSE; Stop it! It's the nuns!

ANTONIO: The nuns! The Sisters! Do you think they'll buy a
    paper?

LUIS: No: they have no money of their own. They have to give it
    away.

JOSE: Good thought: they might give us enough for a drink. On
    your feet!

The MEN *stand and try to look holy as a procession enters. It is led
by* SISTER JOSEPH *ringing her bell, followed by* SISTER
MICHAEL *and* SISTER GABRIEL *flanking* ROSA, *who is
wearing a veil, and the other girls:* ANITA, EVA, JUANITA,
MARIA, NATALIA, RAMONA, *and* ROSALIA.

ANTONIO: Read all about it!

ALL: Shh!

ANTONIO: Sorry!

The procession stops. SISTER JOSEPH *glares at* JOSE *whose face is screwed up.*

SISTER JOSEPH: What's wrong with you, Jose? Hangover again?

JOSE: I'm just feeling holy, Sister.

SISTER JOSEPH: Holy! I've seen pairs of socks looking holier than that! Now, are you men going to join us in prayer before we enter the convent?

JUAN: We've nothing else to do. What are we praying for? Rain? Jobs?

JOSE: Drink?

ALL: Shh!

SISTER MICHAEL: We are praying for this girl who has decided to enter our convent here.

SISTER GABRIEL: A new novice, then there'll be four of us.

SISTER JOSEPH: She is going to become a nun like us, a bride of the Church, away from the temptations of men and drink and money.

PEDRO: I wish somebody would tempt us with money.

JOSE: Or drink.

SISTER JOSEPH: Quiet! Show more respect! Let us pray.
    Almighty God, look down on your humble servant Rosa . . . .

PABLO: Rosa!

ALL: Shh!

ROSA (*throwing back her veil and running to him*): Pablo! When did you get back?

PABLO: Just now.

ROSA: I'd given up hope.

PABLO: Please, Rosa, don't go in the convent. Marry me instead. I love you!

ALL: Aw!!

ROSA: Where have you been these last two years, then?

PABLO: Trying to sail round Africa, haven't I? But all the time I was thinking of you Rosa.

ALL: Aw!

ROSA: Have you brought me a rich gift as a token of your love?

PABLO: Yes, I have.

ROSA: Ooh! Is it gold?.

PABLO: Er, no.

ROSA: I bet it's jewels, isn't it?

PABLO: Erm, no.

ROSA: What is it, then?

PABLO: It is an exotic bird.

> The MEN *try not to laugh.*

GIRLS: Ooh! An exotic bird!

ROSA: Is it a bird of paradise, Pablo, that you have brought as a symbol of your undying love for me? Say it is!

PABLO: It is! Well, actually it isn't. It's more of a . . . sort of a . . . dead parrot. (*He holds it up.*)

GIRLS: A dead parrot!

> The MEN *burst into laughter.*

ROSA: A dead parrot! Is that how much you love me? (*She weeps.*)

GIRLS: Aw!

PABLO: I'm sorry, Rosa, but our ship was wrecked, and the parrot was all I could save. That and one peseta. I taught it to dance the flamenco but it tore a ligament and died.

ROSA: Have you no money to marry me with?

PABLO: Well, not this year, no.

> ROSA *weeps again.*

ANITA: Talk! All talk! This year, next year, never! You men are all the same!

FRANCISCO: I'm not.

ANITA: Oh no? Three years ago you swore to marry me, didn't you?

FRANCISCO: Yes. When I get a steady job.

ANITA: Yes, when! When the moon turns blue and the West is the East. When! That's all I ever hear from you!

> The MEN *laugh.*

GIRLS (*pointing to the* MEN): You're all as bad!

MEN: What, us?

GIRLS: Yes, you!

MEN: Well.

GIRLS (*infuriated*): Ooh, men! (*They fold their arms and stand tight-lipped.*)

PEDRO: Well, we can't get jobs, can we? This town's dying. The crops wither in the heat, we've sailed out for days and caught no fish, and the travellers on the main road all pass us by. We just live on hope.

PABLO: Please, Rosa. We can always hope.

ROSA (*after a pause*): No, I'm sorry, Pablo. I can't live on hope any longer.

SISTER GABRIEL: You're right, Rosa: they'll never marry you. Come on, girls, why not all sign up as nuns? You'll be better off with us.

JUANITA: Why?

SISTER MICHAEL: Because even if the men get jobs as sailors and marry you, they'll be away most of the time, and you'll be always worrying if you'll ever see them again. What sort of life is that? Life in the convent is safe and sure.

PABLO: No! Don't listen to them!

MEN: Please!

JUAN: Do you girls know why they really want you to be nuns? 'Cause they're scared that the convent'll have to close. There's only three of 'em left, and the building's crumbling and they've no money to repair it. If they can get ten nuns, they get a building grant from the Pope, don't they?

LUIS: They get no money from visitors, either.

SISTER GABRIEL: It's quiet and peaceful.

LUIS: So is a tomb. You might as well be dead in a convent.

SISTER MICHAEL: No. They can study.

MANUEL: Study! What use is study to a woman?

The MEN *agree.*

JOSE: A woman's life is cooking and cleaning and bringing kids up. What is there to study?

ROSALIA: Why? Why is that a woman's life?

GIRLS: Yes, why?

MEN: 'Cause it is!

GIRLS: Why??

MEN: 'Cause for!!

ANTONIO: Anyway, it's more fun in the world outside the convent. Life's changing all the time: people are inventing things like printing and marmalade and sherry. Perhaps they'll even discover America!

ALL: America! What's that?

ANTONIO: I don't know: nobody's discovered it yet.

ALL: Aw!

ROSA: Oh! I can't decide what to do. Can you, girls?

GIRLS: No.

SISTER GABRIEL: Sister Michael and I have composed a little song about life in the convent to help you decide. Ready, Sister?

SISTER JOSEPH: What is this song? Is it sacred?

SISTER MICHAEL: No, but it's fun!

SISTER JOSEPH: Fun! Oh, go ahead.

SISTER MICHAEL
SISTER GABRIEL } : Thank you, Sister. A-one, a-two!

> SISTER MICHAEL *and* SISTER GABRIEL *suddenly hitch up their skirts and launch into a song-and-dance number. Tune: 'Any Old Iron'.*

SISTER MICHAEL
SISTER GABRIEL } : It's good fun, being a nun,
Living in the convent.
It's fun singing and saying your prayers:
No-one drinks and no-one swears.
No rough guys to black your eyes
Once you're in the convent.
Come and join the fun now, come and be a nun now:
Come to the convent!

> *The* GIRLS *applaud and the* NUNS *take a bow.*

SISTER MICHAEL: Come along and join us, girls! All girls together!

NUNS: Yes!

PABLO: No! Let's give 'em our recitation, lads! It's called 'You Need a Mate'. Ready? Right!

PABLO: God made Adam and God made Eve:
        Two people, one of each.

PEDRO: And what God said to Noah
        Was not 'Take three or four',
        But couples, one of each.

LUIS: 'Cause that's the way the world is made:
        Not groups of six or eights

MANUEL: Or fives or sevens
        Or nines or elevens

MEN: But twos, 'cause we all need a mate!

FRANCISCO: 'Cause if your life's a muddle
        You can share it with your mate.

ANTONIO: You can have a kiss and cuddle
        If you're married to a mate.

JUAN: A convent may be peaceful
        And the praying may be great

JOSE: But it cannot give you happiness.
        'Cause it can't give you a mate.

MEN: You need a man!
    You need a mate!

The GIRLS *applaud.*

MEN: Come and be a wife!

NUNS: Come and be a nun!
    Choose a quiet life!

MEN: Marriage is more fun!

GIRLS: Decisions, decisions!

ROSALIA: If the men had money, we'd marry them, wouldn't we?

GIRLS: Yes, we would.

SISTER MICHAEL: But they have no money, have they?

GIRLS: No.

SISTER JOSEPH: And no way of making any. Come and join us: you know it makes sense.

The GIRLS *look at each other, nod, sigh and move to the* MEN.

ROSA: The Sisters are right. Goodbye, Pablo.

EVA: Goodbye, Francisco.

All the GIRLS *say goodbye to the* MEN, *who stand depressed as* SISTER JOSEPH *rings her bell.*

SISTER MICHAEL: Follow us, girls!

The procession forms up again and they begin to move off.

COLUMBUS (*off*): Wait! Stop!

They stop. Enter COLUMBUS. *He is a stage Italian, possibly with a curly moustache and a hat like Chico Marx's, shabbily dressed and carrying a bag. He stands panting and wiping his brow.*

SISTER JOSEPH: Have you something to say to us?
(COLUMBUS *nods.*) Then speak out. What do you want?
COLUMBUS (*going up to her, fumbling in his bag*): A Ninety-Nine-a, please.
SISTER JOSEPH: Can't you see where you are?
COLUMBUS: Is a queue? Not a queue? You no gotta Ninety-Nine? All-a right! Choc-ice, wafer, cone-a, whatever-a you got: any sort of ice-a-cream-a. My heart leaps when I hear your bell!
SISTER JOSEPH: We three are Sisters!
COLUMBUS: Family firm, eh? That's-a good! Who's a-serving?
SISTER MICHAEL: No-one is serving!
COLUMBUS: That's a-bad! You no serve-a, you no getta the trade!
ROSALIA: Excuse me, these three ladies are nuns.
COLUMBUS: Nuns! I see! Oh, a thousand pardons. In my country, you ring-a the bell, you sell-a the ice-cream. Is a tragedy. I can't find the ice-cream, I can't find the money, I can't find the men.
PABLO: Men! What do you need men for?
COLUMBUS: To come-a with me! You come-a with me, I make-a you all reech!
PEDRO: Reech! What talk is that? You're not Spanish like us, are you?
COLUMBUS: No, no: I am Italiano. My father, he is from Italia. My mother too. Genoa.
PEDRO: No, I've never met her. I've never been to Italy.
NATALIA: Genoa is a town. A seaport in Italy.

COLUMBUS: Right! A seaport in Italy.

PEDRO: Oh, right! Genoa! Well, be seeing you.

JOSE: Hold on! He said he could make us rich, didn't he?

COLUMBUS: That's-a right-a.

JOSE: I don't believe you could make anybody rich. You're poor yourself.

COLUMBUS: I bet you!

JOSE: How much?

COLUMBUS: Er, one peseta.

JOSE: One peseta! I thought you were rich.

COLUMBUS: How much you got?

JOSE: Well, er, nothing. How about you?

COLUMBUS: Er, somebody lend me a peseta. (ANTONIO *hands him a coin.*) There!

JOSE: You're as poor as we are!

COLUMBUS: I don't care: I'll soon be rich. Anyway, I'm famous: my name's in the paper.

JUANITA: What paper?

COLUMBUS: That newspaper there!

MANUEL: Ah! You're the marmalade man, aren't you? I bet you're going to open a factory to make orange jam, aren't you, mister?

COLUMBUS: Maramalada! Huh! What a stupid name!

JUAN: No, you must be the sherry man! The new drink! You want us to make oak barrels, don't you, mister? We're good at barrel-making, aren't we, lads?

MEN: Yeah!

COLUMBUS: Sherry! Huh! Another stupid name!

FRANCISCO: Hey, you're not the freak, the er, fellow who wants to get to the East by sailing West?

COLUMBUS: That's-a right! That's-a me!

EVA (*scanning the paper*): What's your name, then?

COLUMBUS: Cristobal Colon.

ALL: What?

COLUMBUS: Cristobal Colon.

ALL (*laughing*): Cristabel!

COLUMBUS: Why does everybody laugh at me? I tell-a my plan to the King of Spain: he laughs so loud! I tell-a my plan to the

King of Portugal: he laugh even louder! Why? It's a good plan.

MARIA: It's not the plan they're laughing at: it's your name.

COLUMBUS: My name?

MARIA: Yes. It's a girl's name is Cristabel.

COLUMBUS: Cristobal!

FRANCISCO: It's all the same: you've got to change it. What about Arthur or Fred or Kevin? Or Orville?

COLUMBUS: But all my friend call me Chris.

SISTER JOSEPH: Why not call yourself Christmas?

ALL (*contemptuously*): Christmas!

NATALIA: Christina?

ALL: Nah!

ROSALIA: Crispin! That's a man's name.

EVA: No. Christopher! What about Christopher? That sounds good.

ALL: Yeah!

COLUMBUS: All-a right Christopher Colon.

RAMONA: Colon! You can't call yourself Colon! It's a disease, isn't it?

ROSALIA: No, it's a punctuation mark. Two dots. It's like being called Comma or Full Stop. You can't call yourself after a punctuation mark, especially one meaning two dots: these kings just think you're too dotty to take seriously.

ALL: That's right!

COLUMBUS: Colon is a-funny?

ALL: Colon is a funny, yes.

ROSALIA: Look at that other explorer with the stupid name. Whatsit. Rolo, Solo . . . .

JUAN: Polo.

ROSALIA: Polo, right. What did he discover? Mints with holes and hockey on horseback. With a better name he'd probably have discovered China.

SISTER JOSEPH: I think the most impressive names are Greek or Latin.

ROSA: Yes! Like Julius Caesar!

EVA: Marcus Antonius!

ANITA: Septimus!

JUANITA: Octavius!

NATALIA: Brutus!

MARIA: Enobarbus!

JUAN: Christopher Enobarbus! That's impressive!

COLUMBUS: But all my papers are signed Chris Colon.

RAMONA: All right: Colonbarbus!

LUIS: No: too long.

ANTONIO: Colonbus.

ALL (*thoughtfully*): Colonbus. Colombus. Columbus. Yes!

COLUMBUS: Columbus, Christopher Columbus.

JUANITA: That'll do. The King of Spain won't laugh at you now:
he'll give you the ships you need. And with a name like that
anybody'll follow you. I would.

GIRLS: Yes!

COLUMBUS: No: I only take men. Will you men sail with me?

MANUEL: Sail where?

COLUMBUS: Japan.

PABLO: Er, Japan is in the East, not the West.

MANUEL: Right. You sail West, you fall off the edge of the
world, don't you?

ALL: Yeah, off the edge.

COLUMBUS: No. What shape is the world?

PEDRO: Round. Like a plate.

COLUMBUS: Suppose I told you that it's not round like a plate?
It's round like a ball.

ALL: A ball!

MANUEL: What sort of ball? A Rugby ball?

COLUMBUS: No! Like an Edam cheese.

RAMONA: Well, if it's like an Edam cheese, why isn't it covered
in red wax?

Laughter.

FRANCISCO: Why aren't you covered in red wax? Go on, sir.

COLUMBUS (*producing a globe from his bag*): This is a model of the
world. There's Spain: there's Japan. For years, people have been
going nearly all the way round to reach Japan. But if you sail
West, the other way, I reckon we'll be there in about a month.

MARIA (*raising a hand*): Well, if the world is like a ball, why don't
people slide off it?

COLUMBUS: Why doesn't the moon fall down? Why is it made of green cheese? Why does God permit evil?

ALL *applaud.*

FRANCISCO: If we sail with you to Japan, sir, when shall we get back?

COLUMBUS: Within three months at the outside you will all return laden with gold and pearls and jewels, enough to make your sweethearts into queens!

GIRLS: Queens!

COLUMBUS: Yes! Can you wait three short months for that?

GIRLS: Oh, yes!

SISTER JOSEPH: What about joining us . . . .

GIRLS: No way!

SISTER MICHAEL ⎫
SISTER GABRIEL ⎬ : None of you?

GIRLS: None of us!

COLUMBUS: Are all you men going to sail with me?

MEN: All of us!

COLUMBUS: Splendid! Follow me! Make your farewells!

All the MEN *say goodbye to their* GIRLS.

PABLO: Goodbye, Rosa. We'll soon be back with the gold, then we can marry.

ROSA: 'Bye, Pablo. Look after yourself.

COLUMBUS: Time to go, men! I am your leader now: your captain, your admiral. And what's my name?

MEN: Christopher Columbus!

COLUMBUS: And don't you forget it!

MANUEL: And don't you either.

Laughter.

COLUMBUS: Don't laugh at me! Line up! Stand up straight! Right turn! Eyes forward! Quick march! Left, right! Left, right!

COLUMBUS *and the* MEN *march out.*

EVA (*calling*): See you soon, Francisco! Frankie! See you!

MARIA (*sitting*): He can't hear you. Sit down.

EVA: Why?

MARIA: What else are we all going to do for the next three months?

SISTER MICHAEL: We nuns are going to pray.

MARIA: Well, that's your job, isn't it?

ROSALIA: Me, I'm going to get drunk.

NUNS (*shocked*): Rosalia!

SISTER GABRIEL: What good will that do?

ROSALIA: Cheer me up. Stop me thinking about Pedro drowning on the edge of the world.

EVA: They're not going to drown! They're all going to bring gold back. And pearls and jewels, aren't they? Aren't they?

The others GIRLS *shrug and look doubtful.*

ANITA: I've never met a rich sailor, have you? (*To* ROSALIA) I think I'll join you in a drink.

SISTER JOSEPH: Girls who went to my school, drinking! I never heard of such a thing!

ANITA: You've never heard because you've never listened It was always 'Button your lip, do as you're told and read the Bible'. Well, I read that Christ turned water into wine at Cana. Right?

SISTER GABRIEL: But drinking won't solve your problems.

RAMONA: What problems? It's the men who have problems, not us. Either they drown or they don't. Either they find Japan or they don't. Either they bring back treasure or they don't. Women don't have problems. Not that sort, anyway.

SISTER JOSEPH: We nuns have no problems, have we, Sisters? So much prayer, so much meditation, so much work in the convent garden. It's peaceful.

SISTER MICHAEL: It can be boring. But we do know what we're supposed to do, yes.

NATALIA: That's our problem, isn't it? What are *we* supposed to do? All right, we help bake bread and do the washing and herd the goats, but that's not a full life, is it?

SISTER GABRIEL: You could have become nuns, all of you.

NATALIA: Talk sense!

ALL (*shocked*): Ooh!

NATALIA: Well, how could all girls become nuns? If we did

there'd be no babies born and the whole world 'ud die off, not just this town. (*To* SISTER JOSEPH) Wouldn't it?

SISTER JOSEPH: Er, well . . . .

NATALIA: 'er, well' nothin'! What if the Blessed Virgin had been a nun? There'd have been trouble in the convent, wouldn't there?

Laughter.

SISTER JOSEPH: What a blasphemous thing to say! A good Catholic girl should not have such thoughts!

NATALIA: Well, what thoughts should she have? We're not supposed to think, are we? We're supposed to let old women like you and our mothers do our thinking for us! But they don't think either. You nuns just repeat what you're told to think, and our mothers think what our grandmothers thought. Like parrots!

ROSA: Dead parrots!

GIRLS (*laughing*): Right!

SISTER JOSEPH: So what great thoughts have you all got? Go on: tell me. You say I don't listen: well, now I am listening. What have you to say? Any of you?

Silence. The GIRLS *look at each other.*

SISTER MICHAEL: Perhaps they need a little time to think, Sister.

SISTER JOSEPH: They have all the time in the world.

RAMONA *raises a hand.*

RAMONA: This isn't exactly a great thought, Sister, but there's something I've always wanted to do.

SISTER JOSEPH: Well?

RAMONA: Well, ever since I was a girl, I've always wanted to . . . to . . . ring your handbell.

Laughter.

SISTER JOSEPH (*smiling*): Go ahead.

RAMONA *approaches the bell, picks it up tentatively, then rings it once, smiles, and rings it loudly.* ALL *applaud, smiling.*

SISTER JOSEPH: That puts me in mind of when I was a schoolgirl and I was one of a team of handbell ringers. Very tuneful. I used to dream of playing in St Peter's before the Holy Father. Of course, we weren't allowed.

EVA: Oh, I dream as well.

JUANITA: Don't we all?

ALL (*dreamily*): Mmm.

JUANITA: What's your dream, kid?

EVA: I dream of standing in a big hall with pillars and colours and lights, and I sing to all the people. I'm dressed in gold and all the people applaud. And there's a man.

SISTER JOSEPH: Is it the Holy Father himself?

EVA: No, he's younger. I'd love to be a singer.

ANITA: Do you know what I've always wanted to do? Make pots. We once saw a man in Seville making a pot out of wet clay. It was like magic: his hand moving and the clay changing shape. I told my mother that's what I wanted to do, but she told me not to be stupid, she'd never heard of such a thing.

JUANITA: That's what all the mothers say.

GIRLS: Mmm.

ROSALIA: And all the Sisters.

GIRLS (*smiling*): Mmm.

ROSA: I went to Seville that time, when it was the festival, and a man tried to talk to me and he had fair hair. He was English and he couldn't speak Spanish. And I thought, 'I wish I could talk to him in his own tongue, in English.' I never told Pablo. It must be magic to talk another language.

MARIA: Another dream.

GIRLS: Mmm.

SISTER JOSEPH: Enough of dreams! It's time for us Sisters to pray, so we'll leave you all. Come, Sisters!

SISTER MICHAEL (*who has been whispering with* SISTER GABRIEL): Sister Joseph, could we please talk a little longer with the girls? It's lonely in the convent.

SISTER GABRIEL: Please!

SISTER JOSEPH: Time for prayer is time for prayer! That's the rule. And you have no reason to come outside the convent for another month.

SISTER MICHAEL ⎤
SISTER GABRIEL ⎦ : A month!

SISTER JOSEPH: That's right.

NATALIA: No, it can't be right: talking's good, isn't it?

JUANITA: Yes. I wonder if . . . I'd love to . . .

GIRLS: What?

JUANITA: You nuns know more than we do. You know
   languages and painting and music, but you're just going to shut
   yourselves up again. It's such a waste, when we're all outside
   without our men.

SISTER JOSEPH: You can still change your minds.

GIRLS: No!!

JUANITA: No, we're not cut out to be nuns, Sister. What I
   wondered was . . . well, everybody has dreams, like nuns
   dream of Jesus and Mary and that. And we all have dreams, like
   ringing handbells or learning pottery or English or being a
   singer. I've always wanted to do illuminated letters like in that
   Bible in the convent that you used to show us.

SISTER JOSEPH: We must go in a minute: what are you saying?

ROSALIA (*in one breath*): What she says is why can't we come to
   the convent every day till the men come back and you can teach
   us and we can all live our dreams?

GIRLS (*applauding*): Yes!

RAMONA: And we can chat as we work!

GIRLS: Yes!

SISTER MICHAEL ⎤
SISTER GABRIEL ⎦ : Please, Sister Joseph!

SISTER JOSEPH: Very well, but we must begin every session
   with a prayer.

RAMONA: A very short prayer.

NUNS: A short prayer.

SISTER JOSEPH: Agreed?

ALL: Agreed?

SISTER JOSEPH: Good. Now we must hurry. We shall welcome
   you all tomorrow morning. Come, Sisters!

   SISTER JOSEPH *rings her bell and the* **NUNS** *go out.*

ANITA: Something to look forward to.

GIRLS: Mmm.

MARIA: Stop us thinking about the men.

JUANITA: Nothing stops me thinking about men: that's why I couldn't be a nun.

Laughter.

NATALIA (*who has been looking at the paper*): Tell you what.

ALL: What?

NATALIA: This man in Seville who's invented this marmalade stuff says he's going to open a new factory there soon.

MARIA: So what?

NATALIA: So what I say is this: I'm not going to wait for ever for Luis to come back with the gold. There's a whole world outside this town. I'll study with the nuns for six months, and if the men aren't back in that time I'm going to pack up and go to Seville.

JUANITA: You might not get that job.

NATALIA: I'll find something. It's better than sitting here, isn't it?

ALL: Yes.

EVA: What we learn from the nuns might be useful for getting work.

ALL: Right.

MARIA: Your mother won't like it.

NATALIA: My mother can lump it.

ROSALIA: You're right: I'll come with you.

ANITA: And me. Six months with the nuns, then off to Seville if the men don't come back. All in favour?

The GIRLS raise their hands.

ANITA: Anyone against? No-one.

EVA: I pray that the men do come back.

ANITA: Don't we all? But prayer's not enough: we have to work as well. All meet outside the convent, seven o'clock tomorrow morning, right?

All: Right.

The convent bell begins to ring.

ANITA: See you.
ALL: See you.

    ALL *go out severally except* RAMONA *who stands listening to the bell.*

RAMONA: Hey! P'raps they'll let me ring the big bell! Wow!

    RAMONA *runs off. The lights dim to indicate the passage of time, but the bell continues to ring.*

Scene 2

The lights come up. Enter ANITA *and* MARIA *carrying bundles.*

ANITA: I told the others we'd wait here.
MARIA: You're not taking much with you to Seville.
ANITA: Nor you. One advantage of being poor.

    Enter RAMONA, ROSALIA *and* NATALIA *carrying bundles.*

ROSA: My mother asked me where I was going. I said I was going to get the washing done early.
ANITA: Mine was still in bed.

    ROSA *takes out a book.*

RAMONA: What are you reading?
ROSA: My English course.
RAMONA: You and your English. What good is it?
ROSA: I might meet that Englishman in Seville. Anyway, I've enjoyed studying this last six months since the men went. Haven't you?
MARIA: 'Course I have. Hey, I've finished that flamenco dress for myself. Sister Michael gave me some red satin from an old robe. It looks great. She tried it on herself. (*To* ANITA) You taking any of your pots with you?
ANITA: No, they're too heavy. And all those tiles with the picture of Our Lady. I left 'em with the nuns.
MARIA: That's the saddest thing about leaving the town: we've had such fun learning with the nuns, and now it's ended.

Dressmaking and pottery and cookery and English and signwriting and mixing drinks.

NATALIA: Well, at least we've all done something we've dreamed of doing, not something that our mothers or the Sisters wanted us to do. I've learned some real fancy cooking.

ROSALIA: And what those nuns don't know about mixing drinks! They say it's in case the Pope comes, but I think they're secret drinkers!

JUANITA: I wish the others'd get their skates on: somebody's going to see us.

MARIA: They're saying goodbye to the Sisters.

ANITA: I'm surprised they can hear each other with that bell ringing. It sounds like a funeral.

NATALIA: Sister Gabriel says that she's ringing it because the town's dead now that we're leaving. She was crying.

Enter EVA *and* JUANITA *carrying bundles.* EVA *is wiping her eyes.*

RAMONA: What's the matter? You both look miserable.

JUANITA: Why should we look happy?

RAMONA: Because it's like going on holiday, isn't it? Seville's a great place, a new world for us.

ROSA: The Sisters say they'll write to us if the men turn up.

RAMONA: What, after six months? Seven, nearly. They said three. We all know what's happened, don't we? They've sailed over the edge of the world.

EVA: Don't, Ramona: it's horrible!

RAMONA: We all have to die sometime.

EVA (*standing*): Oh, come on! What are we waiting for? If we're going to Seville, let's go!

ALL: Right.

They stand. The bell stops.

JUANITA: That's the end of this place. Leave it to the nuns and old women. Let's move!

They start to move off.

FRANCISCO (*off*): Eva!
EVA: Frankie!

> FRANCISCO *runs on and embraces* EVA.

FRANCISCO:We're back! All of us!

> *The* GIRLS *scream with relief and happiness.*

RAMONA: Have you all brought dead parrots?

> *Laughter.*

FRANCISCO: You'll find out when the others come. I ran when I heard the bell. Where are you all going?
EVA: I'm not going anywhere now that you're back.
ANITA: Now that you're all back with gold!
JUANITA: And pearls!
NATALIA: And jewels!
GIRLS: Gold and pearls and jewels!
EVA: Can I have mine now?

> *Laughter.*

FRANCISCO: Er . . . Sit down.
EVA: Frankie, where's the treasure you promised?
FRANCISCO: Sit down.

> *They sit.*

FRANCISCO: See, what happened, we sailed West for about a month. Nothing but sea, but Columbus kept saying we were near land, 'cause we saw branches in the water, and landbirds in the sky. Then we sailed through like cornfields.
GIRLS: Cornfields?
FRANCISCO: Sort of yellow seaweed. For miles and miles.
EVA: Frankie, where's the gold? You didn't find any, did you?
FRANCISCO: Just listen. We never knew when we might go over the edge, and some of the sailors wanted to mutiny, but Columbus drove us on. He's a weird bloke: they say he was drunk with the stars. And he promised a big reward to the first man who sighted land.
ROSALIA: Did you find land? Did you reach Japan?

FRANCISCO: Well, we came to some big islands with brown people on. They don't wear clothes there.

NATALIA: Don't tell the nuns!

Laughter.

EVA: Did you sight land first? Were you the lucky one?

FRANCISCO: Nobody was lucky.

ANITA: Why not? Somebody must have seen it first.

FRANCISCO: Yes. He didn't get the reward, though.

ANITA: Why not?

ROSALIA (*looking offstage*): Pedro!

NATALIA: Luis!

Enter the OTHER MEN. *The girls cheer and clap, then run to embrace them.*

FRANCISCO: I'm just telling the girls about that guy who first sighted land.

PABLO: Poor bloke.

ROSA: Why's he poor.?

PABLO: 'Cause Columbus wouldn't give him the reward, see?

LUIS: Said he'd seen it first himself.

EVA: Cheat!

JUANITA: Were they good, these islands you found?

MANUEL: Well, yes, but . . .

PEDRO: They weren't full of gold or spices, were they?

MEN: No.

GIRLS: No gold?

PEDRO: Not much. Columbus traded beads and stuff for some gold, and we sailed round for three months looking for gold-mines.

PABLO: Never found any.

JUANITA: As long as you've got *some* gold: we're not greedy! Show us some.

JOSE: Not here.

MARIA: Go on!

GIRLS: Go on!

Silence. The MEN *look at each other, shrug and start to fumble in their duffel-bags, then they look at the* GIRLS.

PABLO: See, we haven't had the share-out yet.

ROSA: What do you mean?

JUAN: Columbus wants to impress the King and Queen with all the gold we've brought back, so he's keeping it all just for now.

MANUEL: And all the giant seashells and parrots and natives.

RAMONA: Natives! In their birthday suits!

The GIRLS *scream with laughter.*

MANUEL: No, they've got like aprons on, and gold jewellery.

MARIA: Oh, I'd love to see 'em!

GIRLS: Yes!

PABLO: You will. All of you.

GIRLS: When?

PABLO: Tomorrow.

GIRLS: Tomorrow!

PABLO: Yes. Columbus and the King and the Queen are all riding to Seville, and the whole procession will arrive here tomorrow night. We told them where to turn off the main road, and we said they'd be welcome to spend the night here, then he can give us our share of the gold and jewels now that the King and Queen have seen them.

ROSALIA: You must all be crackers! How are we going to lodge the whole of the Spanish court in a town this size?

PABLO: They're used to moving around: they don't live in palaces all the time.

The NUNS *appear, listening.*

ROSALIA: Maybe, but they expect luxury, don't they? Not straw mattresses and wool blankets like we have. They'll have us hung!

SISTER JOSEPH: No, they won't. We've been listening to you, and we can put up the royal party in the convent. We always keep luxury guest apartments ready in case the Pope drops in.

SISTER MICHAEL: The others can stay in your spare bedrooms. They'll be so tired with travelling that they won't notice where they're sleeping.

NATALIA: Especially as we'll get 'em all drunk!

JOSE: What on? We've no money for drink till we get our share of the gold.

ROSALIA: Don't worry: we've a barrel of wine that we've saved up for the day you came back.

SISTER JOSEPH: And we have a few bottles in the convent in case the Pope drops in.

Laughter.

SISTER GABRIEL: And don't worry about the food either. If we all put our backs into it we can have a royal feast on the tables by tomorrow evening. We'll go and light the convent ovens now. See you later.

The NUNS *go out.*

PABLO: Tomorrow we'll be rich!

ROSA: And we can all get married!

PEDRO: Hey! How about a drink to celebrate before we start work?

ALL: Right!

RAMONA: Race you to the cellar!

ALL: Right!

They race off. The lights dim slightly and the convent bell starts to ring quickly. ALL scurry about preparing for their visitors: tables with food and drink are brought on, the NUNS *put up a sign saying 'Welcome to the Pope', with 'Pope' crossed out and replaced by 'King and Queen'. JUANITA puts up a sign saying 'Jose's Bar'. The bell stops and everyone relaxes.*

JUAN: Phew! I'm whacked! It's harder than sailing a ship.

MARIA: Never mind, we're just about ready. I bet the King and Queen'll be really surprised.

RAMONA: They'll probably give us a few extra jewels as tips. Bags me serve at the top table!

ROSA: All tips shared. Agreed?

PEDRO: Nothing to do now but wait.

EVA: I've been wondering . . .

ALL: What?

EVA: I wonder if they'll expect to be entertained?

PEDRO: We've no time to hire entertainers, have we?

NATALIA: We can do something ourselves.

PEDRO: Such as?

NATALIA: A barbecue on the beach.

PEDRO: What, after the banquet?

NATALIA: They eat all the time, rich people: they've nothing else to do. Besides, we need to get 'em out of the way while we tidy up. We can give 'em sardines and lots of drink. Right?

ALL: Right!

ROSALIA: Hang about: it's not as easy as that! We haven't enough wine for the whole court to drink all evening. And they won't give us big tips if we run out of drink.

PABLO: Columbus won't be pleased either.

EVA: We'll have to give 'em orange juice: we've lots of that.

MANUEL: You can't give the King orange juice! He's not a baby! Beside it looks odd, that juice: it's from blood oranges.

ROSALIA: Dump it in the wine!

ALL: What?

ROSALIA: Give 'em the best wine from the convent with the banquet, then tip all the rest in a wine vat.

RAMONA: And the dregs!

LUIS: And the leavings!

ROSALIA: Right. And pour in the orange juice and mix it all up. Tell 'em it's a new drink. Call it 'Sangria'.

ALL: Why?

ROSALIA: Why not? It sounds good. Sangria.

ALL: Sangria.

NATALIA: All right, we'll have a barbecue with whatsit. Ganglia.

ALL: Sangria.

NATALIA: Sangria, right. What else?

SISTER GABRIEL: We should have music.

RAMONA: Aw, not hymns, Sister!

SISTER GABRIEL: Sister Michael and I can sing 'Come to the Convent'.

JUAN: Us lads can dance a hornpipe and sing 'What Shall We Do With A Drunken Sailor?'

RAMONA: I could do a striptease.

NUNS: You could not!

RAMONA: Just an idea.

MARIA: I'll dance a flamenco in my new dress.

RAMONA: Right: I'll accompany you on the handbells.

MARIA: If you must.

ANTONIO: What if the sangria runs out?

SISTER JOSEPH: There is some beer in the convent cellar.
Guinness. In case we get an Irish Pope.

ANTONIO: We'll keep that in reserve.

PABLO: Right! We're ready for anything! All work together, keep
smiling, remember that the customer is always right, and wait
for the tips to start rolling in.

MANUEL: I bet Columbus'll be so pleased that he'll give us the
biggest shares of gold!

ALL: Yeah! Gold!

*Silence. ALL smile at the thought of the gold. A fanfare is heard,
followed by a cheer and circus-type music. ALL stand and look offstage.*

PABLO: They're coming! Put your aprons on and line up!

*ALL scamper round to put on their aprons etc. to serve their visitors,
then they form a line facing the audience, but looking in the direction of
the music. It gets louder.*

PABLO: Smile! Look smart!

*During the following ALL watch as the imaginary procession passes
in front of them. The music still plays, but not loud enough to drown
their voices, which get louder up to 'Barbecue!', then gradually fade as
the procession passes out of their sight and the music also fades to silence.*

EVA: Look! The King and Queen!

PABLO: And that's Columbus there – riding with 'em on his
white horse!

JUANITA: Doesn't he look posh?

PABLO: Yes, he's an admiral now.

RAMONA: Look at the brown people! They're magic!

MARIA: Hundreds of horsemen!

EVA: Red feathers waving!

ANITA: Shining armour! Silver! Gold! Jewels sparkling!

PEDRO: They're coming to our turn-off now! They'll soon be here!

PABLO: Smile!

ALL *smile wide, then their smiles fade.*

JUAN: They've missed the turn-off.

RAMONA: They're keeping on the main road.

ALL: Oh, no!

JUAN (*calling*): Your majesties! Captain Columbus! Admiral! We're here!

ROSA: They haven't heard you.

PABLO: All shout!

ROSALIA: We've got the sangria!

ALL: Sangria!

NATALIA: Barbecue!

ALL: Barbecue!

SISTER JOSEPH: Guinness!

ALL: Guinness!

EVA
SISTER MICHAEL } :Singing!
SISTER GABRIEL

ALL: Singing!

MARIA: Dancing!

ALL (*quieter*): Dancing!

MANUEL (*despairing*): Fun!

ALL (*quiet, gloomy*): Fun.

ROSALIA: Gone.

Silence. ALL *look at their preparations.*

NATALIA: All this good food.

JUAN: And all that good wine wasted making this sangria muck.

ROSALIA: Do you mind?

PABLO: What worries me is when we get our share of the gold.

JUAN: Forget it.

MANUEL: But Columbus promised it.

LUIS: Yes. Like he promised that reward to the first man who sighted land.

NATALIA: You mean, we'll get no gold?

MEN: No.

MARIA: So we still can't get married?

JUAN: No.

Silence. SOME *sit.*

JUAN: No jobs on land: we'll have to look for another ship.

MEN (*gloomily*): Mmm.

MARIA: We'll go to Seville. Try for a job in the marmalade factory.

GIRLS: Mmm.

ROSA: I'll write to you, Pablo.

PABLO: Thanks a lot: I can't read.

ROSA: Oh, I'm sorry, Pablo: I'd forgotten. (*Looking at the food*) What a waste.

RAMONA: We don't have to waste it. Let's have a feast before we part! I'm starving.

ALL: Right!

ALL *prepare to eat.*

SISTER JOSEPH: Wait a minute! Grace before a meal!

Grumbling, ALL *stand.*

SISTER JOSEPH: I'm waiting for silence. Thank you. Close your eyes. That's better. Now, before we say grace let us offer up one final prayer to the Lord to help us. Let us pray. Almighty God, we beseech you to let the light of your blessing shine again on this town. Send your holy angels to give us prosperity so that these young people may be able to marry according to the ordinance of thy holy Church. Amen.

ALL: Amen.

SISTER JOSEPH: Now, bless this food . . .

The sound of a motorcoach is heard. ALL *turn and look in the direction of the road. The noise gets louder and we can hear the passengers singing loudly 'We are off to sunny Spain'. The singing gets louder, the coach stops and the passengers cheer raucously.*

SISTER JOSEPH: Who are these uncouth people?
SISTER MICHAEL: They're the answer to your prayers, Sister!

Enter TOURISTS *carrying luggage.*

TOURISTS: Hey, look at this, kid! Barbecue! Sangria! Joe's Bar! Brilliant! Dump the luggage at the hotel up there. See the sign: 'The Three Nuns'. Then we'll come back here to eat. Hey!

The TOURISTS *go out noisily.*

SISTER JOSEPH: They're not angels!
SISTER MICHAEL: No, they're English, but they'll do.
ROSA: English! Let me make a sign. (*She busies herself.*)
SISTER MICHAEL: The English will eat our food and drink our sangria and come to the barbecue and clap the flamenco and fill all the beds in town, year after year after year.
SISTER GABRIEL: And you can all get married if you can find a spare moment, because the tourists will provide you all with jobs for life. This place will never be the same again: it's a new world! (*Looking up*) Thank you, Lord.
ALL (*looking up and smiling*); Thank you, Lord.
SISTER JOSEPH: What does your sign say, Rosa?
ROSA: It's in English, Sister. It says 'Welcome' in English.

She puts up the sign. It says 'Real English Pub'.

SISTER JOSEPH: Well done! Let's all learn some English to greet our visitors. Say it aloud!
ALL: Real English pub.
SISTER JOSEPH: Louder!
ALL: Real English pub!
TOURISTS (*off*): Real English pub! Hurray!
SISTER MICHAEL: Here they come! Smile!

More cheering from offstage. ALL face, smiling, in the direction of the cheering, holding out their arms in welcome.

[*Curtain*]

Epilogue

ALL:	New World! This is the New World! Right here!
RAMONA ⎱ : MANUEL ⎰	Our old town has disappeared, Blown right off the map.
NUNS:	Tourists bustle and drink their beer Where we used to take a nap.
PABLO ⎱ : ROSA ⎰	Our latest hotel has fourteen floors. No need to take our word because
ANTONIO:	You can read all about it in the paper!
ALL:	Read about the skyscraper!
MARIA ⎱ : JUAN ⎰	And our airport has a brand-new runway For tourists seeking the sunway To holiday happiness funway to the
ALL:	New World!
ROSALIA ⎱ : PEDRO ⎰	We have carparks by the acre for the hordes who make the trip And the harbour's been enlarged to take the very largest ship.
FRANCISCO ⎱ : EVA ⎰	And you may like to record that we've just won the award As the Number One attraction in the whole of Spain,
ALL:	'Cause our town is visited again and again. New World! New World!
JUANITA ⎱ : JOSE ⎰	We've an English pub selling English ale That is swallowed by the gallon by the English male.
NATALIA ⎱ : LUIS ⎰	And we've built a little cafe that is very very shady Selling strawberries and cream to the English lady.
NUNS:	The nuns are getting merry upon convent-bottled sherry That we sell to the visitors in tiny little flasks

ANTONIO ⎤ :   And we are getting richer selling copies of a
ANITA   ⎦   picture
              Costing 2000 pesetas to any visitor who asks
              The price.

ALL: 'Cause everybody's getting their price.

MEN: The sailors are busy rowing anglers out to sea
              To fish for shark or sturgeon.

GIRLS: And their wives are selling piles of expensive
              tiles
              With a genuine picture of the Virgin!

ALL: Life is fizzier: we're all busier
              Than we ever were before.

MEN: And we cannot believe that we ever said

GIRLS: 'We've got to move, 'cause this town is dead'

ALL: 'Cause the New World we were seeking
              Is right here! We're all right here!
              New World!

[*Curtain*]

After 'Astings

CHARACTERS

English	**French**
KING HAROLD	DUKE WILLIAM

English		**French**	
OSBERT		WALTER	
OSMUND	*Knights*	BASIL	*Knights*

GERTRUDE *a Lady*

Ladies
FLEUR

Servants
GURTH
GARTH
EDWARD
EDMUND
EDGAR
EGBERT
HILDA
MATILDA
AUDREY
EDNA
GWENDA
ELFREDA

MARIE
NATALIE
RENEE
CECILE
BLANCHE

MESSENGER

The action takes place in the castle kitchen at Hastings.
SCENE 1: October 1066
SCENE 2: October 1070

Warning
Taking this play seriously could damage your knowledge of history. William *did* beat Harold near Hastings in 1066, but it took 300 years before their two languages finally became one.

French words
There are a few French words and phrases used in the play including:

French	Sounds something like	Means
un je ne sais quoi	ern jerner seh kwa	a certain something
après la bataille	ap-ray la bat-eye	after the battle
ragoût	rag-oo	stew
crache	crash	spit
tout de suite	toot sweet	straight away
bière	bee-air	beer
crudités	crewdeetay	salads
frappé	frappay	iced
haute cuisine	oat kwi-zeen	high-class cooking

You should be able to work out most of the other French expressions. If you have the chance, look through your part before you read it aloud and ask for help if you're doubtful. (When Hilda says 'Silver plate' she means 'S'il vous plaît', meaning 'please', and when she thought that Sir Walter had ordered 'Shoe' he had actually said 'Chou' meaning 'cabbage'.)

But don't worry, even if you don't know much French: the way that people speak both English and French has changed a lot in 900 years, so if you're not sure how to say a word just speak it confidently and keep going. (Probably most other people in the room aren't sure how to say it either, and the play is supposed to be a comedy, after all. Good luck!)

Scene 1

*The castle kitchen at Hastings, October 1066. Two entrances: one to the
outside, one to the dining-room. Tables, benches, plates, mugs, cooking
utensils. GARTH takes something out of a cooking-pot, looks at it
doubtfully then puts it in his mouth. Enter GURTH with a piece of
sacking over his head.*

GARTH: 'Ey up, Gurth. Still rainin'?

GURTH: Teemin' it down. Where's all the women-folk?

GARTH: With that teacher-lady, that Gertrude.

GURTH: Aw. She still tryin' to get 'em to talk posh?

GARTH: Yup. King 'Arold's orders.

GURTH: 'E's up North somewheres, in't 'e?

GARTH: Yup. They say 'e's fightin' them Danes.

GURTH: Well, I 'ope they're 'avin' better weather than what we
    are. I bet 'Astings 'as 'ad more rain this year than anywhere else
    in England.

GARTH: What about 'Arrogate?

GURTH: Where's that?

GARTH: Dunno. Wanna chunk? (*He takes something out of the pot
    and gives it to* GURTH.)

GURTH: Looks a bit raw. Is it ready to eat?

GARTH: Well, 'Ilda said mix all the stuff up, bung it in this pot
    and eat it.

GURTH: Eat it?

GARTH: Yeah. Eat it for 'alf an hour.

GURTH: That's all right then. Let's get eatin'.

    They eat.

GARTH: What year is it, anyway?

GURTH: Ten something.

GARTH: Oh, yeah. Ten sixty something.

GURTH: Four? Five?

GARTH: Could be. Tell you what.

GURTH: What?

GARTH: All this bad weather'll keep the tourists away.

GURTH: Yeah. Good thing. Can't stand the French – they only come for the duty-frees.

GARTH: Six!

GURTH: Six what?

GARTH: 1066! That's what year it is! Two sixes!

GURTH: What's it matter? All years are alike, except some 'ave more rain than others.

Shouting is heard from off-stage.

GURTH: They're 'ere.

GARTH: About time.

Enter EDWARD, EDMUND, EDGAR *and* EGBERT *carrying a barrel which they set down.*

EDWARD: Ale, Garth. Ale, Gurth.

GARTH: 'Ail, Edward.

EDWARD: Nah! Ale: in this barrel. 'Oo likes ale?

ALL: Me!

EDWARD: Right: get suppin'.

ALL *fill a mug.*

EDWARD: I bet there's more ale drunk in this castle kitchen than anywhere else in England.

EDGAR: It's a good sup. 'Ey, this weather'll keep the tourists away.

GARTH: That's what I said.

EDMUND: French! Can't abide 'em! (*He spits.*)

EDGAR: They don't swill ale like real men. What do they drink? Wine! (*He spits.*)

EGBERT: And what do they eat? Frogs! (*He spits.*)

EDMUND: And snails! (*He spits.*)

ALL: Yeucch!

EDWARD: And truffles!

EGBERT: What's truffles, Eddie?

EDWARD: Sort o' fungus. It grows deep down, and them French use dogs called truffle-hounds what grub 'em up, slobberin' all over 'em. Then the French eat 'em.

EGBERT: What, the 'ounds?

OTHERS: Nah, the truffles!

All: Yeucch!

GARTH: 'Ere, 'ave some stuff, all of you.

ALL: Ta.

They take food from the pot and eat.

EDGAR: Tell you summat else: they cook all their meals fancy, them French. 'Erbs an' all that.

EDMUND: 'Erbs! I like meat half-raw. More natural, more better for you.

ALL: Yeah.

EGBERT: Well, why does our king like 'is meat cooked fancy then?

EDGAR: 'Arold? Well, 'e 'as to show 'e's different, dun't 'e? Like the way 'e carries on about sayin' haitches. Anyway, 'e's not 'ere: 'e's up North somewheres.

Enter MESSENGER.

MESSENGER: 'Ail!

EDGAR: In the barrel: 'elp yourself.

MESSENGER: Nah! 'Ail! Greetings! I am a messenger!

EDGAR: Oh, right: what is your messenge?

MESSENGER: My messenge is that our king, 'Arold, 'as won a great victory over the invading Danes at Stamford Bridge.

EGBERT: Where's that, then: Stamford Bridge?

EDMUND: London. Chelsea ground, innit?

MESSENGER: Nah: it's in Yorkshire.

GURTH: Never 'eard of it.

ALL: Nah.

MESSENGER: And now our king is travellin' South to 'Astings.

ALL groan.

EDWARD: What's 'e comin' down 'ere for? Why can't 'e stay in this Yorkshire dump?

MESSENGER: Because 'e 'as 'ad a messenge that the French are getting ready to cross the Channel.

EDMUND: What, in October? In this weather?

MESSENGER: Thousands of 'em are coming, led by Duke William.

ALL: Aw, no!

EDMUND: Not that Duke William! 'E's one of the Norman French: they're worse than the Danes, the Norman French.

EDWARD: 'Ave another drink: cheer us all up!

ALL *gather round the barrel and fill their mugs.*

MESSENGER: I'd better not 'ave another. I'll see if I can find another messenge to deliver.

Exit MESSENGER.

GURTH: Watch out: 'ere's that posh woman!

GERTRUDE *enters as the* MEN *scatter.*

GERTRUDE: Hearken! King Harold is hurrying hitherwards to Hastings!

EDWARD: Right: the messenger just told us. 'Urrying in 'aste.

GERTRUDE: Haste.

EDWARD: That's what I said: 'aste.

GERTRUDE: No, you didn't. What did you drop?

ALL *look around on the ground.*

EDWARD: Dunno: what did I drop?

ALL: What did 'e drop?

GERTRUDE: He dropped his aitches!

ALL: 'Is haitches! Is that all?

GERTRUDE: Is that all? What will King Harold say when he returns to hear you all dropping your aitches?

ALL: Haitches.

GERTRUDE: Aitches! Come in, girls! It's high time for your women-folk to show you their skills in polite speech.

ALL: Oh, no! (*Starting to move*)

GERTRUDE: Stay where you are! Stay! When our noble King Harold arrives here, I want all of you to be sounding your aitches for him like true Englishmen. (*Calling*) Girls!

Enter HILDA, MATILDA, AUDREY, EDNA, GWENDA, *and* ELFREDA. *They stand looking embarrassed.*

GERTRUDE: Now, girls, let's show these chaps how their language should be spoken!

HILDA: We ought to be getting a meal ready.

The OTHERS *agree.*

GERTRUDE: First things first! Line up! Shoulders back! Deep breath! One, two, three!

GIRLS: It's not the hunting with the hounds that hurts the horses' hoofs: it's the hammer, hammer, hammer on the hard high road.

GERTRUDE: Splendid! Men! (*Silence*) Men!

MEN (*reluctantly*): It's not the 'unting with the 'ounds what 'urts the 'orses' 'oofs: it's the 'ammer, 'ammer, 'ammer on the 'ard 'igh road.

GERTRUDE: Oh, the agony! Where are all those aitches?

EDWARD: Aw, why does it matter?

GERTRUDE: It matters because superior people sound their aitches, and we English are superior! Once we strart to drop our aitches, we shall drop our standards, or worse! We shall be no better than foreigners, such as (*pointing*) . . .

AUDREY
EDNA } : The Scots!

ELFREDA
GWENDA } : The Welsh!

MATILDA
HILDA } : The Irish!

GERTRUDE: And . . .

GIRLS: The French!

GERTRUDE: Correct! Who wants to be like the French? (*Silence*) No-one. So, we must work on our aitches. Girls!

GIRLS: In Hertford, Hereford and Hampshire, hurricanes hardly happen.

GERTRUDE: Men!

EDMUND: Count us out: we're not fancy speakers.

MEN: Nah!

GERTRUDE: Then I hope that you do not have to make a speech

to his Highness. I myself have composed an ode . . .

EGBERT: A node? What's a node?

GERTRUDE: Ode! An ode! A poem of welcome to King Harold!
It contains no fewer than 76 initial aitches. The girls are word-
perfect: Perhaps you men would care to join in?

EDGAR: An' p'raps we wouldn't.

GERTRUDE: Faint of heart! Stand tall, girls! Audrey, put that
mug down! All together – one, two!

GIRLS: Hail, hail, Harold, our high and haughty Highness,
  Hail, hail, Harold, the herald of our home.
  Hail, hail, Harold, our handsome, happy hero:
  Heaven hold you hale and hearty, long to hunt and roam.

  In Hastings' hallowed halls and hearths
  His horse and hounds adore him.
  Let hyacinths and hollyhocks and honeysuckles flower!
  Harmonious harps and hunting-horns hosanna before him,
  All hailing and hallooing our happy Harold's power.

The MEN *applaud in an effort to stop them, but they carry on
regardless.*

GIRLS: Hundreds of honeycombs humming with happiness,
  Hundreds of hogs in the mire,
  Hovering birds and horses and herds
  Join in the harmonious choir:

EDMUND: They've said "armonious' once.

GERTRUDE: Shh!

GIRLS: Hail, hail, Harold, our high and haughty Highness,
  Hail, hail, Harold, the herald of our home.
  Hail, hail, Harold, our handsome, happy hero:
  Heaven hold you hale and hearty, long to hunt and roam.
  All hail!

The MEN *look at each other and reluctantly applaud.*

EDNA: What do you think of it?

EDWARD: Well, it's . . . different, innit?

The MEN *agree.*

EGBERT: I wonder if it's not a bit OTT?

MATILDA: What's that: OTT?

EGBERT: Over the top. You know – a bit exaggerated.

GERTRUDE: Exaggerated?

EGBERT: Yes, like calling the king 'andsome and 'appy.

GERTRUDE: *H*andsome and *h*appy!

EGBERT: Yes. I mean no: I mean, well, 'e's not, is 'e? I'd call 'im plain, an' 'e's miserable most of the time, worryin' about French and Danes and that.

HILDA: But 'plain' and 'miserable' don't begin with haitch, do they, you 'alfwit?

GERTRUDE: *H*alfwit, Hilda!

HILDA: Sorry, Gertrude: halfwit.

EDMUND: Yeah, and another thing: what does ''Arold the 'erald of our 'ome' mean?

A trumpet sounds a fanfare offstage.

GERTRUDE: I thought that 'Harold the herald' had a certain ring about it. A certain *je ne sais quoi*.

Enter KING HAROLD, *wearing a crown.*

ALL: The king!

Enter OSBERT *and* OSMUND.

OSBERT
OSMUND } : Kneel before 'is majesty!

ALL *kneel.*

GIRLS: Hail, King Harold!

MEN: 'Ail, King 'Arold.

OSBERT
OSMUND } : Stand!

ALL *stand.*

HAROLD: Hail to you all. As I came in, I heard someone speaking the tongue of our foes, the French. Who was it?

GERTRUDE: It was I, your Highness, but I was only . . .

HAROLD: Silence! Never speak in my presence again!

GERTRUDE: But I have written . . .

OSBERT }
OSMUND } : Quiet!

GERTRUDE (*coming forward*): Your highness, I have written an ode for you with 76 aitches in it. . . .

As she is speaking, the KNIGHTS *bundle her out.*

HAROLD: What an annoying person. By Jove, I'm dry! It gives a fellow an unholy thirst, defeating these hellish Danes.
(EDWARD *gives him a drink.*) Thank you. Tell them about the Normans.

OSBERT: We've had a messenge . . .

EDWARD: We've just been told, sire.

OSBERT }
OSMUND } : Quiet!

OSBERT: We've had a messenge that thousands of Norman French are planning to come across on the ferries. Now, you all know what the French are like.

ALL: Right!

OSMUND: Especially the Norman French.

OSBERT: Right. They'll get boozed up on the boats and then what?

OSMUND: They'll wreak havoc wherever they land.

ELFREDA: And where will they land?

OSMUND: Some say Dover or Folkestone, but I think they'll land further West, somewhere like Eastbourne, or nearer still, at Bex'ill.

HAROLD: *H*ill.

OSMUND: Sorry, your 'Ighness. Highness. Bexhill.

OSBERT: My bet is they'll land right 'ere at 'Astings.

ALL: 'Ere! At 'Astings!

HAROLD: *H*ere! *H*ere! *H*astings! It's not the hunting with the hounds that hurts the horses' hoofs . . .

ALL: It's the hammer, hammer, hammer on the hard high road!

HAROLD: The what?

ALL: Hammer, hammer, hammer!

Pause. HAROLD *finishes his drink.*

HAROLD: In Hertford, Hereford and Hampshire . . .

Enter MESSENGER.

ALL: Hurricanes hardly happen.
MESSENGER: Your 'Ighness!
HAROLD: *H*ighness! Why can nobody speak properly?
MESSENGER: King 'Arold!
HAROLD: Harold! Harold! Harold!
MESSENGER: Yes, sire. The French 'ave landed, sire. Near Bex'ill!
HAROLD: Bex*h*ill! Bex*h*ill! Bex*h*ill! Say it!
OSBERT: Sire, I think we must arm to meet the French.
HAROLD: First things first! All of you: where have they landed?
ALL: Bex*h*ill. Bex*h*ill. Bex*h*ill.
MESSENGER: Sire: we must get there fast.
HAROLD: Where?
MESSENGER: Bex . . . Where you said.
HAROLD: Say it!
MESSENGER: Bex*h*ill.
HAROLD: Good. Well spoken. (*To* OSMUND *and* OSBERT) You two, rally my army. I shall go and pray to God that we may overcome their hated hordes. I'll use a lot of aitches. Hallelujah! Jehovah, Holiest in the height of heaven! Hosanna!

Exit HAROLD, *still talking.* GURTH *blows a raspberry. Laughter.*

OSMUND: Quiet! 'Earken to me. All you men, grab what weapons you can find: bows and harrows, 'alberds, 'ayforks, pick-haxe 'andles, hanything, and follow me to Bex'ill. You women, I want you to make a feast to welcome us back after we've dealt with the French. Not the sort of stuff that Garth serves up, either. Now, move!

The MEN *go out.*

AUDREY: Ooh, 'eck, all them haitches!
GWENDA: Well, we can talk as we like now.

EDNA: 'Ammer, 'ammer, 'ammer.

ELFREDA: Never mind ''Ammer, 'ammer': what are going to make?

MATILDA: Me an' 'Ilda'll bake a cake for afters and decorate it fancy.

ELFREDA: Good idea. I think we'd better make a stew. I know it's not very exciting, but we can keep it warm till they come back.

AUDREY: *If* they come back.

ELFREDA: What do you mean, '*If* they come back'?

AUDREY: You never know with these French: they get up to all sorts of tricks.

GWENDA: But English are better than French any day. Let's go and find stuff to put in the stew.

> *The* WOMEN *go out. The lights dim and we hear voices chanting ''Arold! 'Arold! 'Arold!' then others chanting 'William! William! William!'. They continue alternating, with 'William!' getting louder and 'Arold!' fainter. Finally a loud chorus of 'William!' is followed by a shriek and a solitary, despairing, fading cry of 'Harold!' then a loud cheer from the* FRENCH. *The* ENGLISH MEN *hurry in carrying the body of* HAROLD *with an arrow in his eye. Enter* MATILDA *and* HILDA *who is carrying a cake which says 'English Rule OK' in marzipan on the side.* MATILDA *screams.*

GARTH: Listen! The French 'ave won! We're off to bury 'Arold. You two clear out fast before the French get you. And 'ide this!

> *He gives* MATILDA *the crown and the* MEN *hurry out. Someone off stage shouts 'King William!' followed by a general shout of 'King William!' and a cheer.*

MATILDA: You 'ide the cake and I'll 'ide the crown. Them French'll kill us if they find 'em!

HILDA: No way: watch!

> HILDA *busies herself with the cake. Noises off.*

MATILDA: They're 'ere! Where can I 'ide this?

HILDA: Give it 'ere.

> HILDA *takes the crown, puts it on the cake and steps back. The*

cake now reads 'Frensh Rule OK' Enter WILLIAM *followed by*
WALTER *and* BASIL, *two knights.*

WALTER: Le Roy! The King!

HILDA *and* MATILDA *curtsy shyly.*

HILDA: The new king!
WILLIAM: 'Allo!
MATILDA }
HILDA   } : *H*allo!
BASIL: No! 'Allo, 'allo!
MATILDA }
HILDA   } : Oh. 'Allo, 'allo, your *H*onour.
BASIL: 'Onour.
WILLIAM: 'Allo. 'Onour. 'Ow do you do? 'Ow nice to meet you!
    I crash on your ashes!
MATILDA: That sounds painful!
WALTER: King William says 'e spits on your aitches.
HILDA: That's nice.
FRENCH: Yes, that's nice.
HILDA: Your majesty, we have – 'ave – made a cake for you.
WILLIAM: Ah! Un gâteau!
HILDA: Gateau, yes. A royal cake – look!
WILLIAM (*seeing the crown*): Ah! La couronne!
HILDA: The curown, yes. The curown of England, for you.

She wipes it and presents it to WILLIAM, *saying 'Well done.' The*
KNIGHTS *applaud.*

WILLIAM: Merci.
HILDA: Mercy, yes, your 'Onour.

WILLIAM *puts the crown on.* ALL *applaud.*

WILLIAM: Après la bataille – une feste!
WALTER: After the battle – a feast!
HILDA: A feast, yes! We 'ave a stew – a ragoût – and the gâteau,
    and, er, patties.
BASIL: Petits pâtés.
HILDA: Petty patties, that's right, and ale to drink. Beer.

WILLIAM: Bière! I crache . . .

MATILDA: No, don't crash in the beer, your majesty – it'll spoil it. The dining-room is through there.

HILDA: The feast is coming soon! A la carte! Silver plate! Toot sweet!

The FRENCH *laugh and go out murmuring 'Tout de suite' to each other.*

MATILDA: What's all this 'Silver plate, Toot sweet' rubbish?

HILDA: It's what the French say. We'll 'ave to learn French now, or this new king'll have our 'eads chopped off.

MATILDA: Ooh, I think 'e's nice! 'E's not posh like 'Arold was, is 'e? 'E doesn't sound 'is haitches, for a start.

HILDA: All the same, you'd better brush up your French, ducks. 'Ere, let's take 'em some ale while we get the feast ready.

They fill mugs from the barrel.

MATILDA: What's French for ale, then?

HILDA: Beer, innit?

Off-stage, the FRENCH *start shouting 'Bière' and pounding on a table.*

HILDA: Beer's coming, your 'Onours. A la carte!

MATILDA: Silver plate!

BOTH: Toot sweet!

They go out with the beer. AUDREY, EDNA, ELFREDA *and* GWENDA *hurry in.*

ELFREDA: Where is everybody?

Re-enter HILDA *and* MATILDA.

GWENDA: The French are coming!

EDNA: They won the fight!

HILDA: We know: some are in the dining-room.

GWENDA: Oh, no: they'll kill us! Run!

HILDA: Whoa! There's no running away from 'em.

EDNA: We can 'ide till they've gone.

HILDA: No way: they're 'ere to stay.

ELFREDA: What, to live 'ere?

MATILDA: That's right.

AUDREY: 'Arold won't let 'em.

MATILDA: 'Arold can't stop 'em: 'e's dead. Popped 'is clogs. 'E'll never sound another haitch again, poor beggar.

EDNA: I dunno, I reckon they sound their haitches in 'Eaven.

MATILDA: P'raps 'e's 'appy then.

HILDA: At any rate, 'e can't make us sound our haitches now.

MATILDA: William's our king now, and 'e don't sound no haitches, does 'e, 'Ilda?

HILDA: Not one. Not even in 'haitch'.

AUDREY: So the French are 'ere for good?

MATILDA: Right, and it could be for our good if we play our cards right. Our first job is to give 'em a good feast. A man that's fed well is easier to deal with than a starving one. Right?

OTHERS: Right.

AUDREY: But what about afterwards? We can't feast 'em every day.

MATILDA: We might 'ave to, at that.

FRENCH (*Off*): Bière! Bière!

HILDA (*calling*): Beer, we call it. Coming up!

ELFREDA: I thought they only drank wine.

HILDA: They're getting a liking for beer. Make yourself useful and take some through.

ELFREDA: I daren't! I don't speak French!

MATILDA (*giving mugs to* ELFREDA *and* EDNA): Just say 'Silver plate' and 'Toot sweet' and you'll be laughing! Move!

FRENCH (*Off*): Beer! Beer! Beer!

ELFREDA ⎫
EDNA ⎭ (*calling nervously*): Toot sweet! Silver plate!

They go out and are greeted by a cheer from the FRENCH.

HILDA: No problem.

GWENDA: What are we giving 'em to eat?

ELFREDA *and* EDNA *hurry back in, smiling but flustered.*

MATILDA: All right?
GWENDA: They're ready to eat.

ALL *busy themselves with the food.*

MATILDA: Take the stew in. They call it a ragoût.
ALL: Ragoo.
HILDA: I'll take the cake, the gâteau.
ALL: Gateau.
MATILDA: An' they can eat up those patties from yesterday.
HILDA; Petty patties.
ALL: Petty patties.
HILDA: You're learning fast. Say what you've learned.
ALL: Silver plate, toot sweet, ragoo, gateau, petty patties.
MATILDA: A la carte.
HILDA: You're latching on. In we go!

They take the food into the dining-room and the FRENCH *cheer.*
GARTH *enters from outside but stops when he hears the cheering. The*
lights dim briefly to indicate the passage of time.

Scene 2

The lights come up and GARTH *sits. He takes something from the pot and*
eats it. Enter GURTH *with a piece of sacking over his head.*

GARTH: 'Ello, Gurth: long time no see. Is it raining again?
GURTH: Yeah. Where's the women-folk?
GARTH: Servin' the meal for Sir Walter and Sir Basil and all the
    ladies.

A trumpet sounds.

GARTH: They're starting.
GURTH: Where's the king?
GARTH: Up North somewheres. Taken most of the knights with
    'im to 'arry the Northerners.
GURTH: What's 'at, then – 'arryin?
GARTH: Fightin' 'em, burnin' their villages and killin' their cattle.
GURTH: What's 'e doin' that for? 'E 'asn't 'arried us, 'as 'e?

GARTH: They rebelled, din't they? Said 'e wasn't our king.

GURTH: 'E must be: 'e beat old whatsit, din't 'e? Old 'Arold. Seems years ago. What year is it now?

GARTH: Must be about 1070, I suppose.

BOTH: Mm.

GURTH *takes something from the pot and eats it.*

GURTH: What's this, then?

GARTH: Mouton a la fashion de Paris.

GURTH: Tastes like sheep. 'Ow do you know it's what you said, any'ow?

GARTH: It's all written down 'ere, see? It's what they call a menu, like a list of food in French. All the meals for a week. The women 'ave 'ad a lot of bother, 'cause the French won't learn no English and the women don't know enough French. Like last week the menu said 'Poison'.

GURTH: Poison?

GARTH: Seems like that's the French word for fish. They 'adn't even spelt it right. Another day, 'Ilda couldn't make a word out and she asked what it said and Sir Walter said 'Shoe'.

GURTH: Shoe? You mean, like in 'boot'?

GARTH: Well, what else could it mean? Any'ow, she daren't ask 'im again, so she gets an old shoe and puts it in the pot and simmers it with a carrot and some onions and a few 'erbs. Served it up with dumplin's and cabbage.

GURTH: An' did 'e eat it?

GARTH: Reckon 'e did. Funny thing was, 'e said 'e enjoyed the shoe, but 'e thought the meat was a bit tough.

GURTH: No 'arm came of it, then?

GARTH: No, not like when it first said 'Pain' on the menu: P-A-I-N.

GURTH: Pain?

GARTH: It's their word for bread, but we din't know that. French knight comes into the kitchen shoutin' an' carryin' on an' pointin' at the menu where it said 'Pain'. Red in the face, shoutin' 'I demand the pain!' 'Course, 'e said it funny, but old Edric says 'Pain you want, sir, and pain you shall 'ave.' An' he stamped on

'is foot real 'ard. 'E 'ad 'is clogs on. Broke three bones in the
knight's foot. Shouldn't 'ave done it.

GURTH: Where's 'e buried?

GARTH: In the midden.

*Off-stage, a woman's scream from the dining-room is followed by
shouting. The* ENGLISH WOMEN *enter looking angry.*
GWENDA *is crying and holding her cheek.*

GWENDA (*to* EDNA): I blame you!

EDNA: You asked me what it meant, but I don't know all the
French words.

Enter the ENGLISH MEN *from outside.*

EGBERT: What's wrong?

EDNA (*pointing to the menu*): What's that say, there, on today's
menu?

EGBERT (*studying it*): Crudities. What did you give 'em?

AUDREY (*giggling*): It wasn't what she gave 'em: it's what she did.
(*She whispers to* GURTH *and* GARTH, *who laugh.*)

GURTH: That sounds like crudity to me.

AUDREY: Trouble was, 'is wife was sitting next to 'im, and she
let out a scream. I wish 'Ilda were 'ere.

Enter HILDA *with a basket.*

EDMUND: She's 'ere.

HILDA: Here we are: fresh vegetables for the crudités.

GWENDA *lets out a howl of despair and weeps.*

HILDA: Whatever's wrong?

ELFREDA: One of the knights slapped her face.

HILDA: Whatever for?

EDNA: You see, you weren't here, and you keep saying we ought
not to be frightened of French words, so Gwenda asked me what
I thought crudities meant, and I told 'er, and she went up to one
of the knights and . . . and . . .

She whispers to HILDA, *laughing, and all the* WOMEN *laugh
except* GWENDA, *who scowls. Enter the* FRENCH LADIES:

BLANCHE, FLEUR, MARIE, RENEE, NATALIE *and*
CECILE. BLANCHE *sees* GWENDA, *points at her and launches
into a gabble of angry French. The* OTHERS *keep up a chorus of
'Oui' and 'Scandaleuse!' The* ENGLISH *shout back 'Leave 'er alone!'
'You and your crudities!' and 'Why don't you learn to talk proper?'*

HILDA: Shut up! Quiet! Silence!

Enter WALTER *and* BASIL, *who points at* GWENDA.

BASIL: Elle!
GWENDA: And 'ell to you an' all! 'Ellfire and damnation, I say!
ALL: Ooh!
WALTER: Sir Basil complains that this woman 'as insulted 'is
wife, and 'e demands that she be punished.
FRENCH: Oui! Punie!
GWENDA: An' wee an' puny to you. I'm stronger then 'er! I crash
in your crudities, I do! (*She spits.*)
FRENCH: Ah!
GWENDA: Well, 'oo's to know that crudities meant salad? If
you'd written salad, or veggies, or worts, or wurzels, we'd 'ave
known what to serve, wouldn't we, girls?
ENGLISH WOMEN: That's right.
WALTER (*suddenly understanding*): Ah! Crudités!

He jabbers in French to the OTHER FRENCH, *who say 'Ah,
crudités!' Then* BASIL *jabbers in French, and they* ALL *say 'Ah, oui'
and laugh.*

WALTER: Now we compre'end what 'as 'appened, but it must
not 'appen again. This female must be punished, and all you
English must start to learn French. Tout de suite.
FRENCH: Oyez, oyez!
ENGLISH: Oh no, oh no!
HILDA: If you punish 'er, you'll 'ave to punish all of us, because
it's not 'er fault. We're cooks, not professors!
ENGLISH: 'Ear! 'ear!
WALTER: We shall punish 'er! Now, serve the meal!
GURTH: Serve it yourself!
ENGLISH: Yerr!

WALTER: What is this?

HILDA: This is a strike!

FRENCH: A strike!

ENGLISH: Yes, a strike!

HILDA: It's a word you'd all better learn, now! Toot sweet!

BASIL (*drawing his sword*): We could kill you all!

AUDREY (*stepping forward*): Go on, then! Kill me first! But remember: I'm the only person in England who can cook a soufflé properly. You all enjoyed that lemon soufflé yesterday, didn't you?

FRENCH: Oh, magnifique! (*They mime ecstasy.*)

AUDREY: Manny Feek. Thank you: better late than never. So kill me if you like, but you'll live on soggy soufflés if you do.

FRENCH: Soggy soufflés! Ah, non!

AUDREY: Ah, oui!

GWENDA: I could 'ave done you a lovely crispy salad if you'd told me proper, in English.

NATALIE: English is not our language: we are French!

GURTH: So when are you going home to France, then?

BASIL: Go home? Never! This is our home! England is now our homeland!

EDGAR: Well, if England is your homeland, you must be English. French live in France, English live in England, don't they? (*Speaking slowly*) You – voo – English. We – noo – English. (*Gesturing to all in the room*) We – noo . . . What's 'all' in French?

ELFREDA: Toot.

EDGAR: 'Toot' – right! (*To the* FRENCH) we – noo – toot English now. So you should all learn English because you are English and we could understand you and serve you better. Compree?

WALTER *gathers the* FRENCH *round and explains what* EDGAR *has said.*

GARTH: Well said, Edgar: you put it to 'em straight.

ELFREDA: I liked the way you said 'Compree'.

EDGAR: Well, you 'ave to learn a bit of their lingo, don't you, to get along, like?

WALTER *and the* FRENCH *finish their conversation. Everyone in the room is chattering.*

WALTER (*clapping his hands*): Mesdames et messieurs! (*The* FRENCH *fall silent.*) Peasants! (*The* ENGLISH *glance at him say 'Charming!' and continue talking.*) Ladies and gentlemen!

ENGLISH: Thank you!

WALTER: We 'ave agreed not to punish anybody! (*The* ENGLISH *cheer.*) And we agree that we are now English, but we do not agree to speak like you. We think that everyone should speak like us.

EDNA: But England is our country: we should decide!

(*The* ENGLISH *agree.*)

BASIL: No! It's ours! We won it at the Battle of 'Astings!

MARIE: We 'ave the power! We are your superiors, and we make the laws. So we say 'Speak French!'

(*The* FRENCH *agree.*)

FLEUR: Also French is a superior language. It is the only language for poetry!

EDMUND: 'Ang on! I know poetry! Get an 'earful of this: it's one of me own:

A Norman by name of Duke Billy
Got stuck in the snow and felt chilly.
They said 'Are you 'appy?'
'E said 'No, I am frappé:
I've an icicle hung . . .

EDWARD: Whoa! Stop it: you'll offend the ladies again.

ELFREDA: What's 'frappé' mean, Edmund?

EDMUND: Means 'frozen', dunnit?

Meanwhile, WALTER *is translating the limerick for the* LADIES, *who squeal with laughter.*

BASIL: All right, you 'ave some comic poems in English, but which is the better language for us all to speak to each other?

FRENCH: French!

ENGLISH: English!

FRENCH: French!!
ENGLISH: English!!
FRENCH: French!!!
ENGLISH: English!!!

Silence. The two groups glare at each other.

WALTER: We seem to 'ave reached an impasse, a cul-de-sac, an . . . 'Ow do you say it in English?

AUDREY: Dunno. What does it mean?

WALTER: Well, it means there is nowhere to go. We are stuck.

EDMUND: In the snow. (*Laughter.*)

AUDREY: We don't 'ave a word meaning that. There's always a way out of every problem isn't there?

WALTER: But 'ow can there be a way out for us? One side 'as to win, isn't that so?

FRENCH: Oui.

ENGLISH: No. Could be a draw.

WALTER: Draw? You mean, make a drawing?

GURTH: Nah! 'E means like in football. What's the French for football?

BASIL: We don't play it, so we don't 'ave a word for it.

WALTER: So we don't 'ave a word for a draw, either.

GURTH: Well, 'ow can English blokes talk a tongue that 'as no words for football? It's what we talk about mainly.

GARTH: An' ale, an' women.

GURTH: An' ale, an' women, right.

RENEE: Ale! English 'as no words for good cookery, for haute cuisine.

GURTH: Cookery! We 'ave masses of words, like eat and turnip and, er . . .

GARTH: Cabbage, carrot, dumplings, and, er . . .

GURTH: Turnip, eat . . .

GARTH: Dumplings, carrot, cabbage . . .

GURTH: Suet pudding!

ENGLISH (*nodding*): Suet pudding!

FRENCH (*contemptuously*): Suet pudding! Yeucch!

ENGLISH: Well.

NATALIE: What are the English words for omelette, for soufflé, for quiche, for mousse, meringue, profiteroles . . .

GURTH: We don't need words for foreign muck! We've got all the words we want for good old English food, 'aven't we? (*The* ENGLISH *shake their heads.*) 'Aven't we?

ELFREDA: No, this lady's right. We've learned to eat a lot better since the French came, and you 'ave to know the names of what you want to cook, don't you?

ALL *the* ENGLISH *except* GURTH *and* GARTH *agree.*

CECILE: So, we are agreed that we all speak French?

FRENCH: Oui.

HILDA: No! You 'ave words that we need, agreed, but we 'ave words that you need.

EDMUND: Football and cricket.

EDGAR: Referee and fair play.

EDWARD: Camping!

EDNA: Pullover.

AUDREY: Weekend.

WALTER: Weekend! That's a new idea!

EDWARD: Think about it.

BASIL: We are getting nowhere fast! We 'ave to talk the same language: which one, French or English? It must be one or the other.

MATILDA: Why? These new dishes of yours aren't just one ingredient, are they? Some cook 'as said 'I wonder what'll 'appen if I break some eggs and whisk 'em up and chuck in an 'andful of this and a pinch of that and cook it all and garnish it with grated cheese and a few 'erbs?' You French are so good at making up new dishes! So what I say is, let's cook up a new language! Mix up all the French words and all the English words! The more words, the more ideas, and the more ideas the better!

WALTER: It might not work.

HILDA: Nothing venture, nothing gain. What do you say?

ALL *agree.*

GARTH: We'd better start now. You kick off.

BASIL: Kick off? We kick you?

GARTH: We'll 'ave to teach you football, I can see that. No, you start: tell us a French word.

FRENCH: We say infant.

ENGLISH: We say child.

FRENCH: We say savage.

ENGLISH: We say wild.

FRENCH: We say chant.

ENGLISH: And we say sing.

FRENCH: We say royalty.

ENGLISH: But we say king.

ENGLISH: We say big.

FRENCH: And we say grand.

ENGLISH: We say ask.

FRENCH: But we demand.

        We say profound.

ENGLISH: We say deep.

FRENCH: We eat mutton.

ENGLISH: We eat sheep.

ENGLISHMEN: That fair-haired girl –

FRENCHMEN: Ah, oui, that blonde –

ENGLISHMEN: Will she answer?

FRENCHMEN: Or respond?

ENGLISHMEN: She's so pretty

FRENCHMEN: She's so glamorous

ENGLISHMEN: She's so loving

FRENCHMEN: She's so amorous.

        Offer her a salutation

ENGLISHMEN: Or give her a greeting.

FRENCHMEN: Then arrange a rendezvous

ENGLISHMEN: Or set up a meeting.

FRENCHMEN: And en route

ENGLISHMEN: On the way

FRENCHMEN: She may say oui.

ENGLISHMEN: She may say yea!

ALL: 'Cause whatever way you look at it
    We've got to live together.

ENGLISH: A feather might be called a plume,
FRENCH: A plume might be a feather.
　　　　French and English make one people.
ENGLISH: We all make one folk.
FRENCH: We must learn to talk together
ENGLISH: And even share a joke.
ALL: So let's stir up our languages,
　　　Whate'er our place of birth,
　　　To make our two tongues into one –
　　　The best one on the earth!

　　ALL *cheer, then shake hands with each other.*

MARIE: We French ladies enjoy learning English, and we 'ope –
　　hope – that you will also enjoy learning French.
AUDREY: Thank you. I suppose I should say 'Mercy'.
ELFREDA: You seem to be learning our tongue very sharp.
RENEE: Sharp? A sharp tongue?
EDITH: Fast.
FRENCH: Ah, fast.
BLANCHE: Well, we 'ave a little secret – we 'ave . . .
FRENCH: *H*ave.
BLANCHE: Pardon. We *h*ave a lady to 'elp – *h*elp – us in studying
　　your language.
ENGLISHWOMEN: Oh!
FLEUR: Yes, already we 'ave . . .
FRENCH: *H*ave.
FLEUR: Have learned the useful phrases, such as . . .
BLANCHE: How is your husband? I hope he has henjoyed his
　　holidays hin the Highlands?
RENEE: Hold hard my hand: Hi ham hafraid hof highwaymen.
NATALIE: In Hertford, Hereford and Southamptonshire,
　　hurricanes hardly happen.
EGBERT: That sounds familiar!
EDNA: If you're going to speak like normal folk, you can forget
　　the haitches.
FRENCH: What?
ENGLISH: Forget the haitches!
FRENCH: The aitches!

ENGLISH: Forget 'em! Drop 'em!

Enter GERTRUDE. *The* ENGLISH *groan.*

GERTRUDE: Drop our aitches? Never! Now that our conquerors have become our fellow-countrymen, we can all speak the same glorious language, sounding our aitches together, man and woman, English and French, rich and poor! All together!

FRENCH: It's not the hunting with the hounds that hurts the horses' hoofs: it's the hammer, hammer, hammer on the hard high road! (*They clap excitedly.*)

GERTRUDE: Well done, French folk! But where were the English? Let's hear you again! It's not the hunting with the hounds that hurts the horses' hoofs, it's . . .

ENGLISH (*half-heartedly*): The 'ammer, 'ammer, 'ammer . . . (*Their voices trail away.*)

WALTER: What is wrong?

EDWARD: We shan't be doing much 'untin' with the 'ounds, shall we?

EDMUND: And if an 'ard 'igh road ever gets built, we shall be breakin' the stones for it, not ridin' 'orses on it. What do you say?

ENGLISH: Right!

EDNA: So count us out, Gertie, 'cause workers don't 'ave the breath to spare to sound haitches.

ELFREDA: You can teach haitches to the posh folk. (*To the* ENGLISH) Can't she?

ENGLISH: That's right.

MARIE: You mean, we can have your aitches?

ELFREDA: Take 'em: you're welcome to 'em. Never used: good as new.

FRENCH: Thank you very much!

ENGLISH: You're welcome!

FLEUR: And I've been thinking about the menus.

ENGLISH: Oh, yes?

FLEUR: Yes. I think they look so much better in French. After all, nearly all the dishes are French, aren't they?

NATALIE: You are so right, Fleur: these English just don't have words for omelette, or soufflé, or mousse, or . . .